MW00615214

A map of the Korean Peninsula and Northeast Asia made and printed in the Netherlands in the 18th century.
Written in French and Dutch. It divides the Korean Peninsula in 8 parts.
This is where the Korean expression "Eight provinces" originated. Seoul Museum of History.

A fabulous view of Cheonji Lake in Mt. Baekdusan. Cheonji is the lake at the peak of Mt. Baekdusan (2750m). Located at the far North of Korea, is the highest mountain of the peninsula and the "father" of all the mountains in Korea.

Majestic view of Mt. Baekdusan Valley seen from its peak. This valley was formed by a volcanic explosion and melted glaciers.

Fish fossils discovered in Pohang, Gyeongsangbuk-do Province.

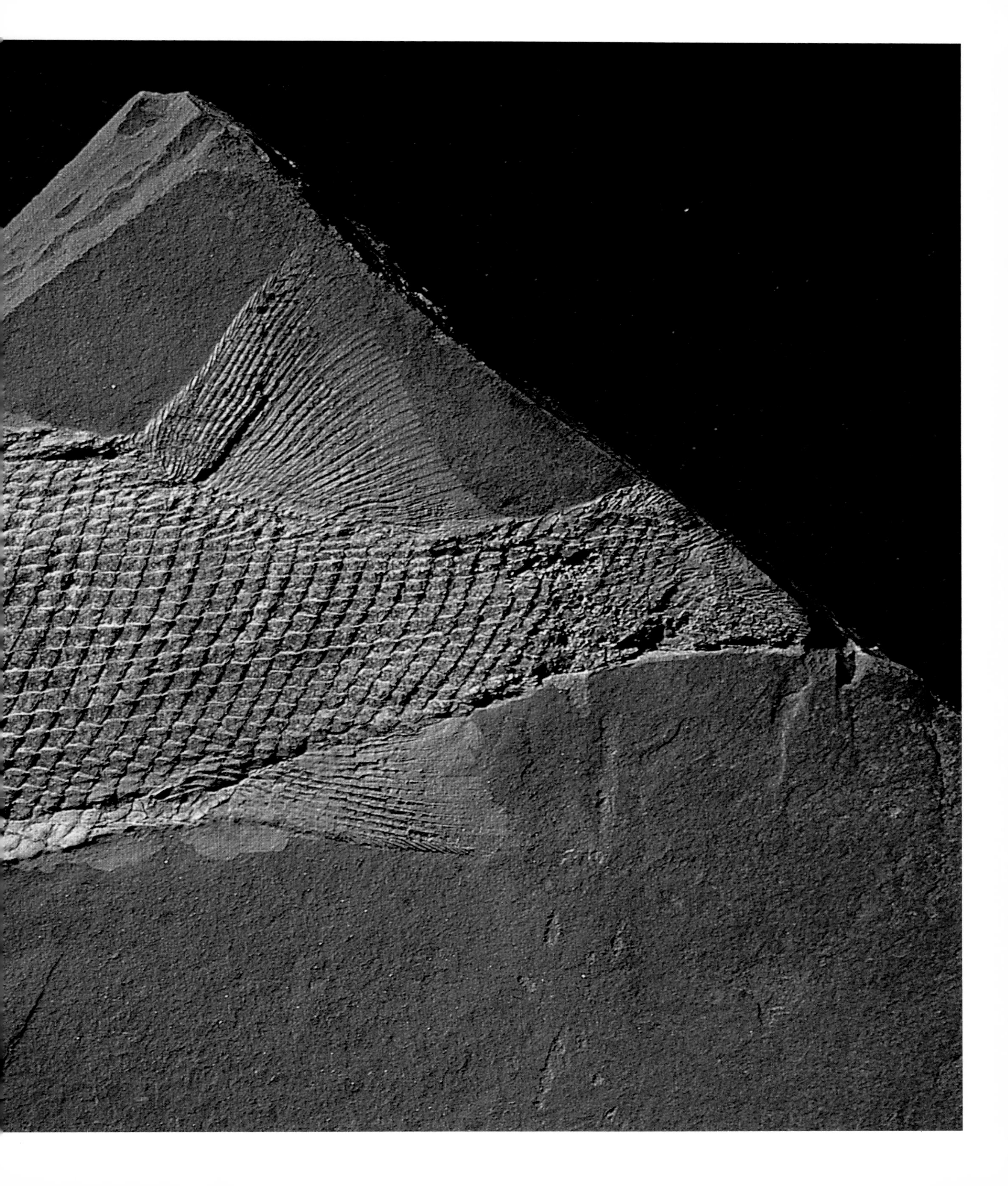

The seating main Buddha in Seokguram Grotto, Gyeongju (8th century). This monumental figure contains architectural, arithmetic, geometrical beauty as well as religious and artistic spirit and has been designated a World Heritage by UNESCO.

Geumdongbangasayusang, gilt bronze Buddha sitting in meditation. A 90 centimeter high Buddha statue from the Baekje Kingdom(18 BC-660 AD) considered to be the best Buddha figure sculpture in Korea. National Treasure No. 83.

Details of ascending dragons on the Seongdeok daewangsinjong(Sacred bell of The Great King Seongdeok), a bell made in 771 during the Silla Kingdom (57 BC-935 AD), weighing almost 19 tons. National Treasure No. 29.

Paik Nam June's video art expressed in a ceramic. The mural seen at the top is a work of Korea University Professor Jin Yeongseon.

Poster of "Old Boy", a film by director Chanwook Park. This movie won the Grand Prix at the 2004 Cannes Film Festival.

oldboy

a **Chanwook Park** film

("JSA", "Sympathy for Mr. Vengeance")

Wildly enthusiastic Red Devils cheering on. Red Devils is the name given to the Korean National Football Team fans.

Be The Reds!

Door and window frames boast superior carving skills and beautiful flower patterns.

The Discovery of Korea

History ▪ Nature ▪ Cultural Heritages ▪ Art ▪ Tradition ▪ Cities

Text by Yoo Myeong-jong ▪ Photo by Kwon Tae-kyun

Discovery media

A recreation of Ilwol-o-akdo. Ilwol-o-akdo was a traditional painting of the Joseon Dynasty containing the sun, the moon and five mountain peaks.
It was used often as the background painting for the King's royal throne. This motif is also used in folding screens.

Contents

Stone lamps (National Treasure No. 17) and Anyangru Pavillion (meaning 'entrance to heaven') in Buseoksa Temple(National Treasure No. 17) in Yeongju, Gyeongsangbuk-do Province. This 1,330 year-old temple is considered to be extremely valuable for Buddhist history as well as oriental architecture and art history.

Preface

Before a minister called William Griffis published a book entitled "Korea, The Hermit Nation" in 1882, Korea was a country veiled in mystery to the rest of the world. Many people didn't even know that a nation called Korea existed. This was the case for many Westerners, who were physically distanced from Korea. For them, Korea was a nation that existed only in legends and myths. Through William Griffis, Koreans were able to meet Westerners but unfortunately this was an "incomplete meeting" because William Griffis wrote his book without actually visiting Korea. He wrote it while staying in Japan, based on books and materials he found there.

The second person to introduce Korea to the West was a British geographer called Isabella Lucy Bird (Bishop), the first woman elected to the Britain's Royal Geographic Society. After visiting and surveying Korea four times from the winter of 1894 to the spring of 1897, she published a book called "Korea and Her Neighbors". This book is a fairly detailed account of Korea one hundred years ago. Bird narrates about various topics including politics, nature, industry, customs, education and religion with a very affectionate point of view.

Thirty years later, an Indian poet called Rabindranath Tagore introduced Korea to the world once more. He called Korea, "the land of the morning calm". He also left us a poem that speaks about Korea. An excerpt from that poem called "The Lamp of The East" goes: In the golden age of Asia, Korea was one of its lamp-bearers, and that lamp is waiting to be lighted once again, for the illumination in the East.

How is Korea viewed by foreigners? The first thing that will pop into some of their minds is probably the Korean War and the division of North and South Korea. Others may be reminded of the dynamic images of the football fans during the 2002 World Cup. And yet others may discover Korea through Korean manufactured cars, televisions and mobile phones. It's true. The images of Korea recorded by William Griffis during the late 19th century are Korea and the nation discovered through its mobile phones is the exact same Korea. However, these are merely minor fractions of Korea. The beauty of Korea is ever more diverse, vast and deep. The image of Korea is far more unique, abundant and enchanting.

This book was made to give foreign readers an intact view of Korea, describe its identity and give insights into its internal beauty. This is the reason the book is divided into history, nature, cultural heritages, art and tradition and cities. In Korea, there is a saying that goes, "you can see only as much as you know". I hope when this book lands on the reader's hands, he or she will be able to discover the abundant beauty of Korea.

Numerous people have helped us write this book. We thank fashion designer Lee Younghee and photographers Seo Jaecheol for kindly providing us with photos we forgot to prepare at the last minute. We would like to send our appreciation to local government offices such as the Jejudo Island Provincial Office as well as several corporations such as Hyundai Asan. We would also like to thank furniture designer Songjaemin, poets Lee Jihae and Choi Hayeon, translators Un He Paik and Debora Paik, and graphic designer Park Youngmee. They have always provided ourselves have also us with fresh ideas and invigorating inspiration. While making this book, we discovered a new enchanting Korea. We would like to dedicate this book to all our ancestors, the creators who have endowed us with the charming 5,000-year old history of Korea and have made us feel this charm again.

Writer **Yoo Myeong-jong**
Photographer **Gwon Tae-kyun**

History

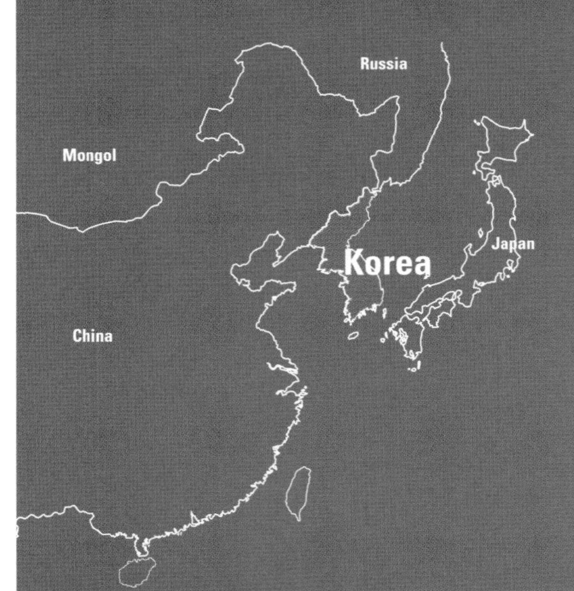

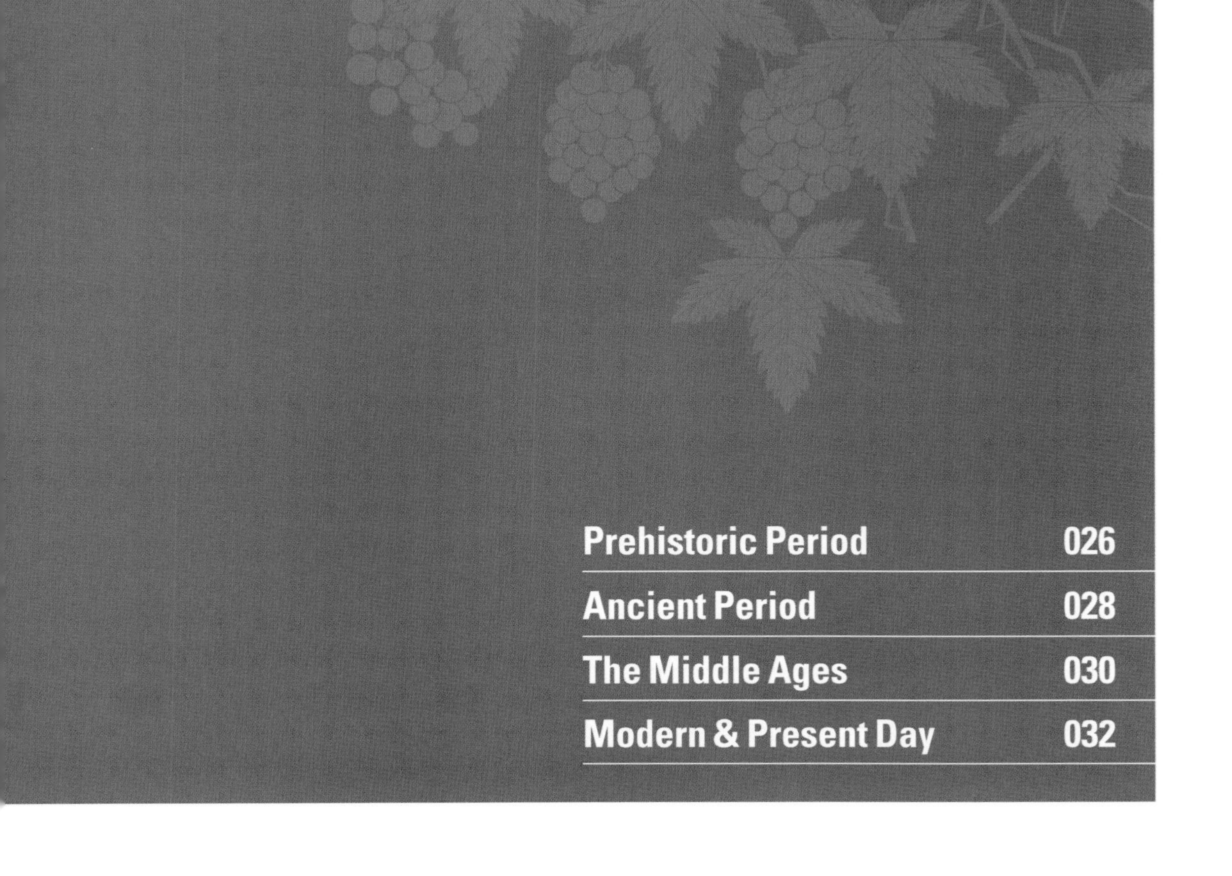

Prehistoric Period

1. Stone daggers and stone spearhead.

The Paleolithic Age and the Stone Ax

Humans started living in the Korean Peninsula around 500,000 years ago. This period is called the Paleolithic Age (50,000 – 5,000 BC). The surrounding environment of Korea during the Paleolithic Age was very different from that of today. The Korea Strait separates Korea and Japan today, but back then they were one connected piece of land. The Yellow Sea that lies between Korea and China was made of land and lakes. Remains from these times have been found in both Pyongyang and Onggi-gun, located in Hamgyeong-buk-do Province, North Korea and in South Korea's Gongju, Chungcheongnam-do Province. They have also been found in Cheongwon-gun, Chungcheongbuk-do Province and Bukjeju-gun in Jejudo Island. The stone ax is a crucial artifact indicating that humans from the Paleolithic Age inhabited in Korea. The inhabitants from the Paleolithic Age in the Korean Peninsula formed communities and survived by hunting, fishing and gathering vegetables. They were the first inhabitants to make and use fire.

The Neolithic Age and the plain-pattern pottery

The Neolithic Age in the Korean Peninsula started 5,000 years ago (5,000 – 3,000 BC). The most representative remains are pottery and artifacts with geometrical patterns. The typical pottery of this period is called the comb-pattern pottery, that was excavated throughout the North, Middle and South of the Korean Peninsula. Just as the Paleolithic Age, the inhabitants of the Neolithic Age formed and lived in communities. They also used primitive methods of farming. Archeologists believe that the inhabitants of the Neolithic Age are the origin and roots of the current Korean race. Relying on this theory, we estimate that the origins of the Korean race had started approximately 7,000 years ago.

The Bronze Age and Dolmens

The Bronze Age began 3,000 years ago (3,000 – 100 BC) in the Korean Peninsula. The most typical remains of this era are the plain-pattern pottery, bronze dagger, bronze ax and dolmens. Farming methods during the Bronze Age were far superior than those established during the Neolithic Age. This period was also the transition point from a matriarchal society to a patriarchal society. A gap began to take shape between the wealthy and the poor, which was measured with each family's amount of production. During the Bronze Age, the wealthiest person became the leader of the tribal society. The division between the ruler and the ruled began to appear in this Age. The dolmens are historical proof supporting the existence of a powerful ruler in this society. Hundreds of dolmen, or tombs of rulers, can be found all over the Korean Peninsula. These dolmens are representative remains of the Bronze Age and were designated a World Heritage by UNESCO.

Gojoseon, the first tribal federation

Samgungryusa, a famous book that accounts the ancient history of Korea has a record of Gojoseon (2333 – 108 BC). According to this book, Gojoseon was a nation founded in 2333 BC by Dangun who was called the "Son of Heaven". Gojoseon was initially founded in the Northeastern region of China or current Manchuria but later moved its capital city to North Korea's Pyongyang. Gojoseon was the first independent tribal nation established around the time the Bronze Age reached its cultural peak. Gojoseon had a basic legal code that prohibited eight types of behaviors, among them fighting, stealing and killing. When these rules were broken, the criminals received punishment accordingly. Gojoseon ruled over Manchuria and the Northern region of the Peninsula for 2,000 years. Later in 108 BC, it was invaded by China's Han Dynasty and disappeared from history.
After the fall of Gojoseon, Manchuria and the Korean Peninsula were divided into and ruled as several tribal nations. This period was called "Period of Many Nations". A century later however, these countries gave way to more powerful ancient nations and also vanished from history.

2. Comb-pattern earth pottery.
3. Stoneware made by ground stones.
4. A depiction recreating ancient cave life.
5. Dangun, founder of the Gojoseon Kingdom(2333-108 BC).

BC 500000	First Peking Ape Man
BC 40000	First Cro-Magnon Man
BC 20000	Altamira Cave wall paintings are painted
BC 4300	Mesopotamian civilization emerges
BC 3100	Ancient Egypt nations are formed
BC 2500	Indian civilization, China's Huanghe civilizations emerges
BC 1700	Compilation of Code of Hammurabi, Babylon
BC 1450	China's Shang Dynasty's Oracle Bone Script
BC 1200	The Trojan Wars
BC 624	Birth of Buddha
BC 588	Buddhism is created in
BC 552	Birth of Confucius
BC 508	Democracy emerges in Athens, Greece
BC 500	The Greek Parthenon is completed
BC 221	Qin Dynasty unifies China
BC 213	China, Emperor Qin Shihuangdi burns books and buries scholars alive
BC 206	Foundation of China's Han Dynasty begins
BC 73	Roman Empire, The Slave Revolt of Spartacus, the Gladiator

Ancient Period

1. Goguryeo mound wall painting depicting a hunting scene.

The Three Kingdoms and Buddhism

Around 100 BC, a new type of nation more powerful than the tribal nation appeared in Manchuria and the Korean Peninsula. There were three such powerful nations: Goguryeo Kingdom(37 BC– 668 AD) located in Manchuria and the northern part of the peninsula, Baekje Kingdom(18 BC– 660 AD), established in current Seoul, and Silla Kingdom (57 BC– 935 AD), established in Gyeongju at the southeastern part of the peninsula. Because these three nations coexisted, this period is called the Three Kingdoms Period(18 BC– 660 AD). A few historians include Gaya Kingdom(42– 562), a small nation made up of allied tribes located in the southern coast of the peninsula and call this period the Four Kingdoms Period.

Around 400, Goguryeo became the most powerful nation in East Asia. Around 427, Goguryeo moved from China to the warmer Pyongyang, a city located in the Northern part of the peninsula. Goguryeo accepted Buddhism from China in 372. However, the Korean commoners felt more comfortable with the various gods of Taoism than those of Buddhism. That is why historians call Goguryeo the "Nation of Gods". Goguryeo is also a nation of mural paintings. There are many mural paintings still remaining inside the burial grounds and tombs in China and near Pyongyang. Through these paintings we can see how the world through the eyes of the people of Goguryeo, their way of living, and calculate their cultural and artistic level as well as their science and technology level. The tomb paintings are time capsules that vividly show us the history of this powerful nation that ruled over east Asia.

While Goguryeo was a kingdom that accepted Taoism as the general creed, Baekje was a Buddhist nation. Baekje adopted Buddhism from China in 384, changed and developed it further, and made a prominent Buddhist kingdom. Baekje was a very open-minded nation which traded with most nations in the current Indochina Peninsula and also carried out a lot of commercial trade with Japan. Baekje is a cultural nation that achieved well-balanced development in academic studies, art, science and religion. They had also achieved a high level of metal and ceramic craftsmanship and impressive sculpture techniques. At around 640, Baekje was able to build a 20-meter high 9-storied stone pagoda and a 60-meter high 9-storied wooden pagoda, astounding historians with their excellent architectural techniques. Baekje also played a bigger role in passing on many of their best academic skills achievements, books, science, architecture and ceramic to Japan and greatly aided it in developing its own primitive culture.

Silla was a weaker nation than Goguryeo or Baekje. Silla possessed many hills and mountains but very little arable land so its farming production was not as high as its counterparts. Until 400, Silla relied heavily on Goguryeo and at times grew alliances with Baekje to keep the nation safe. In 562, Silla took on Gaya, a nation which had already succeeded in unifying several smaller nations, and with this its power grew quite strong. Finally, Silla used Buddhism to

unify its own country and made an alliance with China's Tang Dynasty to conquer Baekje and Goguryeo, succeeding in unifying all Three Kingdoms.

The North-South Nation Era

Through the unification of the Three Kingdoms, northeast Asia began the North-South Nation Era (late 600 – early 900). Silla conquered all of Baekje and a part of Goguryeo's territory. At the same time, the descendants of Goguryeo established a new nation in the north section of the peninsula and Manchuria called Balhae (698 – 926).

Unified Silla thrived greatly creating a synergy effect acquired when the internal energy collected during the unification process of the Three Kingdoms encountered the high-level cultures of both Goguryo and Baekje. The wonderful cultural heritages from Silla's old capital city of Gyeongju were created after the unification of these Three Kingdoms. The most representative heritages are Bulguksa Temple and the Seokguram Grotto.

Since the unification, Silla began to expand its international trading range. It traded not only with China and Japan but also with Arab merchants who came from distant places such as the Arabian Peninsula. Silla became a wealthy kingdom through its trade. There were some royals and nobles who lived in houses painted with gold paint. However these luxurious homes of the ruling class were built of the pain and suffering of the common people. In addition, these gold-painted houses were just signs of the downfall of the ruling class. The extravagance, corruption and monopolization of power by the ruling middle class brought an end to the 1,000-year rule of the Silla Kingdom in 935.

The Kingdom of Balhae was started by Dae Joyeong, a descendant from Goguryeo. This nation took hold of the northern part of the Korean Peninsula and most of Manchuria. Balhae was a strong at that time and was called "the Prosperous Pation of the East" by the people of the Tang Dynasty in China. According to China's historic records, the people of Balhae owned many books and enjoyed reading and writing. These records prove that the people of Balhae were very mature and cultured. Balhae disappeared from history 230 years after its foundation.

2. Sarira casket of Gameunsa Temple in Gyeongju.
3. Balhae relics of animal shapes.
4. Bunhwangsa Stone Pagoda in Gyeongju built during the Silla Kingdom.
5. Samjonbul Image Carved on Rock Surface in Seosan, Chungcheongnam-do Province, also known as "Baekje's Smile".

BC 27	Roman Empire rule begins
1st century	Christianity begins
270	Japanese Yamato Imperial rule begins
280	Jin unifies China
313	Roman Empire makes Christianity official religion
375	Migration of Germanic Tribes begins
395	The Roman Empire is divided into east and west
439	China's Nan Bei Chao Dynasties are formed
476	Fall of West Roman Empire
538	Japan, adopts Buddhism from Baekje
579	Birth of Mohammed
589	Sui Dynasty unifies China
610	Islam is founded
618	T'ang Dynasty is established
771	Charlemagne unifies the Franks
829	The Kingdom of England is established
862	The Russian Empire is established
907	Fall of Tang Dynasty
916	Liao Dynasty established by the Khitan Tribe

The Middle Ages

1. Leaf detail of a Goryeo Dynasty cheongja or celadon porcelain.

2. Jikji, a book printed in 1377 containing the essential words of Buddha and great monks.

Goryeo, the first unified nation

Goryeo Dynasty(918-1392) was the first unified nation in the Korean Peninsula. Before the 10th century, more than two nations coexisted in the peninsula, but after this period, only one nation remains: Goryeo. Just like Silla, Goryeo's official royal creed was Buddhism. However, while Silla's Buddhism was centered on royals and nobles, Goryeo's Buddhism was a new type of Buddhism. It was focused on mental discipline and the people's welfare. It was called *Seonjong* or Zen Buddhism.

The Goryeo Dynasty witnessed a more rapid development of pottery and printing technology then in previous other periods. Proofs of these are the Goryeo celadon, metal printing blocks and the Tripitaka Koreana. The celadon, with their excellent well-balanced beauty and jade color depicts the elegance and fine beauty of the Goryeo Dynasty. A book called Jikji made from Goryeo metal prints is preserved to date. Jikji is the world's oldest existing book printed with metal blocks. The Tripitaka Koreana(or complete collection of Buddhist scriptures) is a book printed from 80,000 wooden blocks. Janggyeong Panjeon storing these wooden blocks were designated a World Heritage by UNESCO.

Goryeo was a nation of powerful clans. These clans seized power in each region of the country and a part of them were politicians in the central government. As time went by, the monopolization of wealth and power by a few rulers turned into a contradictory world of corruption and alienated the common people. As these contradictions grew, the downfall and eventual ruin of the Goryeo Dynasty began. However the name of the nation still remains. *Korea*, the name of the country used worldwide derives from the name *Goryeo*.

Joseon Dynasty

In the late Goryeo Period, General Yi Seonggye unified the alienated reformist scholars and politicians, overthrew the Goryeo Dynasty and established a new nation called Joseon Dynasty(1392-1910).

The Joseon Dynasty is different to Goryeo in two aspects. First, it distanced itself from Buddhism and accepted Confucianism as the new moral system for its society. And second, in order to stop the inheritance of powerful posts, it established a civil service examination and selected civil workers with well-rounded intelligence and culture of two groups: civil or scholar officials(munin) and military officials(muin). These civil and military officials where called yangban (scholar-official gentry). Yangban represent the two ruling class groups, which is why Joseon was also called a yangban society.

When it comes to culture, Joseon was completely different from Goryeo, the previous dynasty. This is because in 1446 King Sejong created the Korean alphabet or Hangeul. Before the creation of Hangeul, all historical records and literary works were written in Chinese characters. Back then, Hangeul had a phonetic language but it did not have its

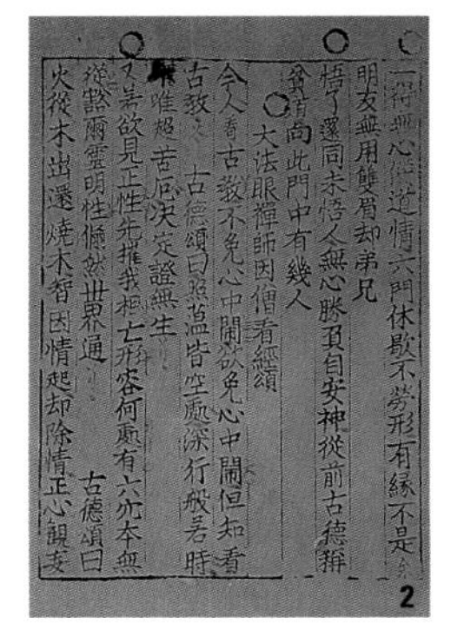

own written form of language to record it. The culture during the Joseon period started developing rapidly as soon as it created its own language. Chinese was the language for the cultured and educated minority while Hangeul was the language of the common people. Hangeul played a critical and decisive role in developing the culture, education, literature and philosophy of this period.

In the mid Joseon period, it was invaded by neighboring Japan. This was called the Imjin Waeran(the Japanese invasion, 1592-1597). Japan started a war to dispatch the powerful military forces of it's feudal lords, seeking political stability domestically and to suppress the power of the rising merchants. The Joseon government could not deal with the invasion properly due to its own conflicts between the conservative and reformist parties. As a result, 70 percent of the territory was occupied at one point. Fortunately, the brilliant operations commanded by the famous admiral Yi Sunsin and the active participation of patriotic volunteer soldiers, Joseon was able to fight the Japanese forces. The impact and damage to Joseon caused by the Imjin Waeran wars was immense. Many palaces and cultural heritages were damaged and due to repercussions of the war, the agricultural productivity decreased considerably. On the other hand, gifted ceramists and potters from Joseon were forced to go to Japan. These artisans established the foundation of Japan's ceramic culture. Japan also adopted Joseon's advanced technology and developed their printing techniques based on it.

During the late 19th century, Joseon underwent great political and social changes. Externally, it traded extensively with advanced European nations and the United States. Internally, it experienced the Gabo Farmer War(1894), a war against the ruling feudal lords and resistance against Japanese interference in domestic matters. This war, where 200,000~300,000 farmers and young educated people participated, was suppressed by the Japanese army. After Japan claimed victory in the Russo-Japanese War in 1904, it removed the Korean Emperor from his throne because he had resisted Japan's aggressive policy and dispersed his army. Finally in 1910, Joseon disappeared from the world map.

3. Goryeo cheongja or celadon porcelain.
4. Portable sundial and compass.
5. The Hunmingjeongeum, a book that contains the philosophy behind the creation of the Korean language and explains its use. National Treasure No. 70.
6. Yi Seonggye, founder of the Joseon Dynasty.

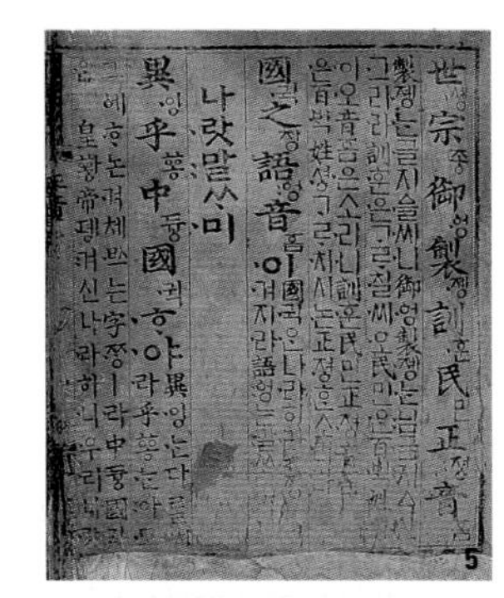
世宗御製訓民正音
國之語音이
나랏말ᄊᆞ미
異乎中國ᄒᆞ야

1096	Crusaders (-1270)
1026	Genghis Khan unifies Mongols
1215	England's Magna Carta is written
1271	China's Yuan Empire is established
1299	Travels of Marco Polo is published
1339	England-France Hundred Year War (-1453)
1368	China, start of Ming Dynasty
14th	The Renaissance begins (-16th century)
1450	Johannes Guttenberg invents the movable printing press
1453	Fall of East Roman Empire
1492	Columbus discovers route to America
1517	Martin Luther's Protestant Reformation
1642	The Puritan Revolution
1644	Qing Dynasty unifies China
1688	The Glorious Revolution
1760	Britain begins the Industrial Revolution
1765	James Watt invents the steam engine
1776	US Declaration of Independence is signed
1789	French Revolution begins
1818	Birth of Karl Marx
1861	US Civil War (-1865)
1863	Abraham Lincoln abolishes slavery
1868	Japan, Meiji Restoration
1869	Inauguration of the Suez Canal
1896	The first Summer Olympic Games
1905	First Russian revolution

Modern & Present Day

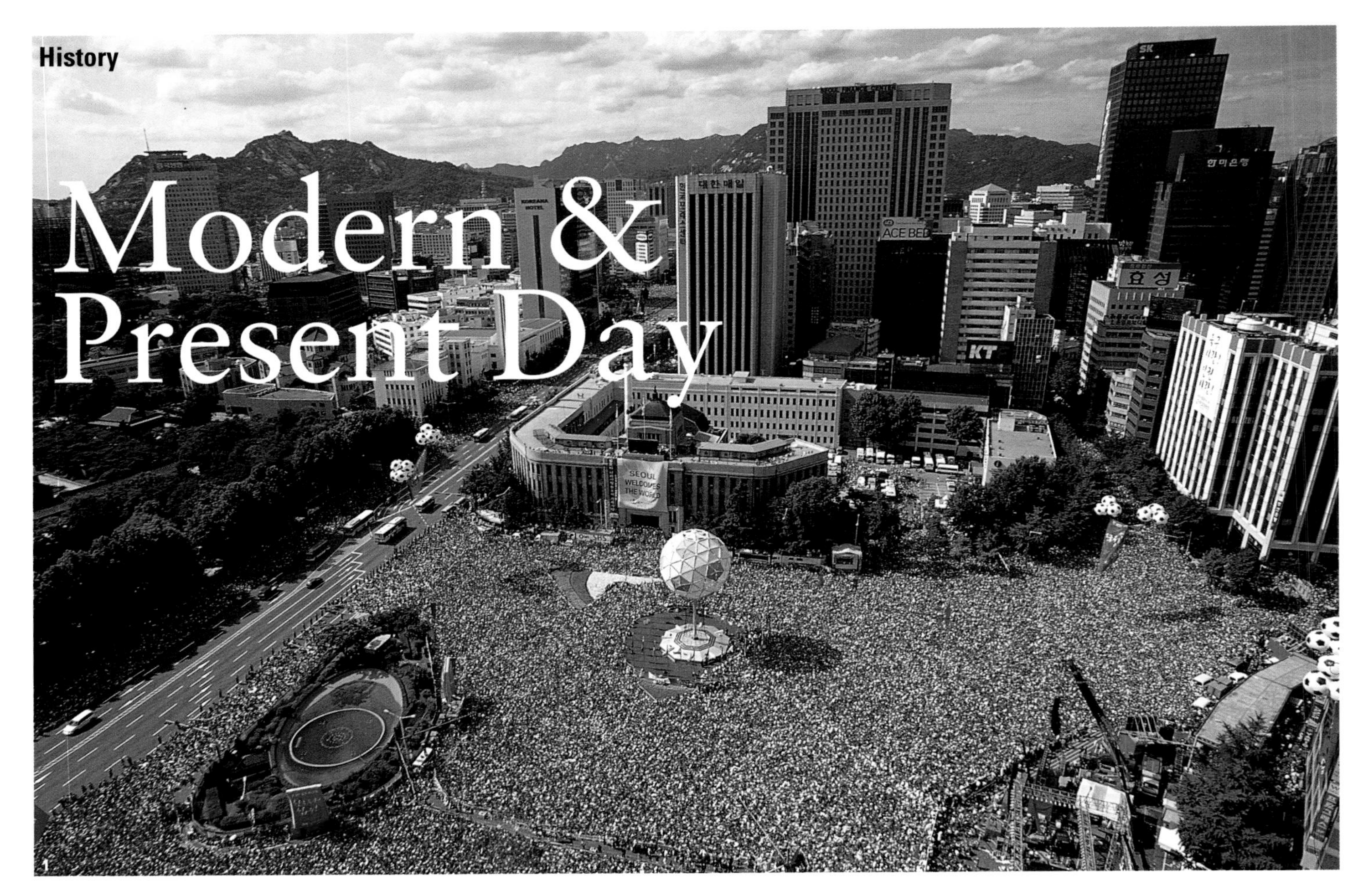

1. Seoul Square filled with cheering football fans during the 2002 FIFA World Cup.

Japanese Colonial Period

Japan forcefully ruled Korea for 36 years since 1910. Japan deprived Korea of several rights and the freedom of assembly, association and press. They forced nationalist newspapers to stop printing and banned all intellectual meetings. Korean people were not permitted to speak or write in their own language. All Koreans were forced to change their names to Japanese names. Many farmers left their homelands and escaped to Manchuria to avoid exploitation and raids. Nationalist intellectuals exiled to China and Manchuria to avoid Japanese oppression.

Since early 1919 until Liberation day in 1945, Koreans in Joseon and Koreans living in Manchuria, China and the United States organized independence movements. The manifestation of the Independence Movement that started on March 1, 1919 had a great impact on Japan. More than two million people participated and it lasted twenty days. This was one tenth of the population at that time. The Japanese military police started shooting indiscriminately at the crowds in the manifestations. They arrested and tortured anyone who stood in their way. 7,509 people died in the manifestations, 15,951 were injured and 46,948 were arrested by the Japanese police.

After these incidents known as the March 1st Independence Movement, with the exception of a few leaders who broke away from the independence movement and cooperated with the Japanese. The majority of the nationalists and socialists continued with their national liberation movements within Joseon and China. Leaders such as Kim Ku gathered nationalists in Shanghai, a city where most political exiles took refuge, established a provisional government and laid out a more structured liberation movement for the libertion of their homeland.

On the other hand, Japan, who had already started the Pacific War, forced 200,000 Joseon men to be drafted and join the Japanese army and forced another 200,000 to work in coal mines and war ammunition factories. They even made barbarous acts such as demand young women to serve as comfort women, sending them to war fronts in Japan, Manchuria, the Philippines, Guam and Saipan. However the end to these invasions, exploitations, oppression, torture and violations of human rights was tragic. In August 15, 1945, after the atomic bomb fell on Hiroshima and Nagasaki, the Japanese Emperor emerged to officially declare their surrender to the Allied Forces.

This tragic and mournful event put an end to the Japan's

invasion in Korea, leaving an unforgettable scar in the hearts of both the Koreans and Japanese.

Separation and Unification Campaign

Korea was liberated from Japanese rule but within three years it experienced another tragedy: the nation was separated into South and North. Political forces supported by the US gained power in the South and the ones assisted by Russia gained power in the North. In 1950, the Korean War began due to North Korea's invasion of the South. The clash between different ideologies was the reason the Korean War started. The peninsula became a site of ruins due to this tragic war. However, South Korea's economy developed enormously since the 1960s. Economists call "Compressed development" this type of economic development that has witnessed no precedents and has rarely been seen since then. And the world calls South Korea's economic development "the miracle of the Hangang River". Based on this rapid economic development, South Korea was able to host the 1988 Summer Olympic Games in Seoul and co-host the 2002 FIFA World Cup with Japan.
South Korea has grown to become the 12th economic power in the world. Korea still maintains its 1~5 rank in the world in the fields of automobile, shipbuilding, semiconductor and construction industries. Since the late 1990s, Korea has also grown to become a powerful digital industry nation.
After the Kim Dae-jung Administration took power in 1997, South and North Korea put the era of conflict and confrontation behind, marking a new beginning for the age of reconciliation and cultural exchange. Particularly after the South-North Summit Meeting held in Pyongyang in June 15, 2000 of the proposal of then president Kim Dae-jung gave the people of the South and North hope for reunification. Afterwards, the tightly shut doors to the skies, the ground and the sea were opened. Now people of the South can visit Mt. Geumgangsan and can fly by plane to Pyongyang. Regular meetings for separated families from the South and North have been made possible. President Kim Dae-jung was awarded the Nobel Peace Prize in 2000 because of his highly praised outstanding hard work towards easing the tension in northeast Asia and opening the age of reconciliation for the South and North.

2. Dokribmun, or Independence Gate, was built in 1897 to show the Korean people's will to protect their right of autonomous rule against foreign invaders.
3. Dockside filled with Hyundai automobiles waiting to be shipped abroad.
4. The first South- North Summit Meeting held after the division of the Korean peninsula, which took place in Pyeongyang, June 15, 2000.

ⓒHyundai Motors

ⓒKOIS

1914	World War I starts
1917	The October Russian revolution
1920	The League of Nations is formed
1922	Italy's Benito Mussolini gains power
1929	The Great Depression
1931	The Manchurian Incident
1933	Adolf Hitler gains power of Germany
1939	World War II starts
1941	The Pacific War (-1945)
1945	The United Nations is established
1949	The People's Republic of China is established
1961	USSR sends first manned spaceship to space
1969	Apollo 11 lands on the Moon
1975	End of the Vietnam War
1980	The Iran-Iraq War (-1988)
1989	China's Tian'anmen Square massacre
1990	Reunification of Germany
1991	Collapse of the Soviet Federation
1994	The EU(European Union) is formed
1996	Cloned sheep Dolly is born
1997	Great Britain hands over Hong Kong to China
2001	Completing of the first human genome map US attacks Afghanistan
2003	US begins attacks on Iraq

Nature

Baekdusan Mountain

Mt. Baekdusan has been more than just a mountain to the Korean People. The first nation to appear in the history of the Korean Peninsula was Gojoseon or Ancient Joseon, an ethnic community that grew its roots in Mt. Baekdusan. Koreans believe that Mt. Baekdusan is the root of the Korean race and the home of the Korean spirit.

© Seo Jaecheol

1. Winter scenery of Mt. Baekdusan's Cheonji (Heavenly Lake).
2. Snow-covered Mt. Baekdusan .
3. Spring scenery of Mt. Baekdusan's Cheonji (Heavenly Lake).

When Moses lead his people to escape from Egypt through the Sinai Peninsula, Mt. Horeb was the symbol that gave an identity to all of them in their journey to their conquest of the Promised Land. Moses received the Ten Commandments from God in it and from then on it has been revered as a "holy mountain".

Similarly, Mt. Baekdusan is admired by people living in the Korean Peninsula, Manchuria and the rest of Northeast Asia. In other words, it possesses the same meaning as that of Mt. Horeb. The first nation to appear in the history of the Korean Peninsula was Gojoseon or Ancient Joseon, an ethnic community that grew its roots in Mt. Baekdusan. Until now, Mt. Baekdusan has been more than just a mountain to the Korean People. Koreans believe that Mt. Baekdusan is the root of their race and the home of their spirit. In this sense all year round, people climb Mt. Baekdusan in search of their roots. This mountain is more sacred than that of the common unconsciousness. Mt. Baekdusan is majestic and beautiful beyond imagination.

Mt. Baekdusan started appearing in historical archives after 200 AD and since then has been given various names in many geography and history books. The reason of the name Baekdusan (literally 'white head') is because of two reasons: first, the color of the stone at the mountaintop is white. And second, except for summer, the peak of the mountain is covered with white snow. Mt. Baekdusan has many other names or nick-names. Most of the names have to do with words related to white, big, long, majestic or sacred, in other words, it is decorated with the noblest words. One example is the nickname "Mt. Taebaeksan." Here "Tae" stands for "big," but is an oriental philosophical concept where the word 'big' is not limited in space but is also related to a historical concept. Mt. Baekdusan is a sacred mountain of the ethnic community that allows the Korean People to look back at their lives.

Mt. Baekdusan is a dormant volcano that merely 100 years ago was an active one. Volcanoes started erupting in Mt. Baekdusan around 2.6 million years ago. Mt. Baekdusan was creaed through a slow process after a huge volcano erupted 550,000 years ago. This eruption created a crater and this volcano stayed active until a hundred years ago. The hot boiling magma underneath the surface shot up creating a 2,750 meters high majestic mountain. It also created the world's highest, largest and most beautiful volcanic lake - 2,189 meter above sea level, a circumference of 14 kilometers, a diameter of 4,5 kilometers, and deepest water depth of 384 meters. Koreans call this lake Cheonji (Heavenly lake). It is a primitive and natural lake of jade green color. If pterosaurs were said to fly over the lake waters, there would be nothing strange about it.

The waters falling from Cheonji create the Jangbaek Waterfalls, a wonderful show of nature itself. Jangbaek Waterfalls is a 68-meter high waterfall located in a U-shaped valley, formed that way due to glacial activity. The water currents which flow all year round, never freeze not even at -30°C. Many visitors praise this waterfall describing it as "a silk-like waterfall." It is said that if you stand under this

3

ⓒ Seo Jaecheol

4

waterfall, your body and soul feel entirely cleansed. In fact, if you are feeling fatigue, visit a hot spring nearby Jangbaek Waterfalls. The waters of the hot springs at the edge of Mt. Baekdusan carry various minerals and have excellent effects in curing illnesses.

In 1980, this mountain was declared International Nature Protection Area by UNESCO. Animals such as tigers, Asian bears, and martens live here. Also rare trees such as minsong pine trees, yew trees (*Taxus cuspidata*), ash trees (*Fraxinus mandshurica*) and rare plants such as mountain ginseng and youngji mushrooms (*Ganoderma lucidum*) can be found here. Mt. Baekdusan's plants and flowers are generally large, bright-colored and have a strong aroma. This is a survival mechanism to attract as many bees as possible which are not so plentiful.

The weather in Mt. Baekdusan is very unstable and often cloudy. As a result, seeing Cheonji on a clear day is a fortunate event. Since ancient times, Koreans have said that three generations must do good deeds to see Cheonji on a clear day. Those who enjoy an adventurous visit, should go to Mt. Baekdusan in the wintertime. Otherwise climb it between July and September when the weather gets warmer.

4. Jangbaek Waterfalls originate from Cheonji (Heavenly Lake).
5. Open air natural spa found at the mountainside of Mt. Baekdusan.
6. Mt. Baekdusan, as seen looking up from middle of mountain.

Baekdu daegan - The backbone of Korean mountains

You must know 'Baekdu daegan' to understand Korean mountains entirely. Baekdu daegan is the enormous mountain range found along the Korean Peninsula shaped like a human backbone. This 1,600 kilometer long mountain range begins at Mt. Baekdusan located near the East Sea coast and is connected to Mt. Jirisan. This mountain range has 12 smaller mountain ranges branching out at intervals to the west side. Baekdu daegan is the backbone and these smaller mountain ranges are its rib bones. Most of the famous mountains in the Korean Peninsula are part of this Baekdu daegan mountain range. Starting from the north are Mt. Baekdusan, Gaema Highlands, Mt. Geumgangsan, Mt. Seoraksan, Mt. Odaesan, Mt. Taebaeksan, Mt. Sobaeksan, Mt. Songnisan, Mt. Deogyusan, and Mt. Jirisan.

1

Hallasan Mountain

If we are allowed to generalize, Mt.Baekdusan is masculine and Mt.Hallasan is feminine. If Mt.Baekdusan is a masculine mountain that carries a superb beauty, Mt.Hallasan reminds us of a mother embracing the plateau. Of all the thousands of mountains Korea has, only these two have beautiful volcanic lakes at the top. And they are also the highest mountains of South and North Korea respectively.

If we consider the Korean Peninsula to be a text, Baekdusan, the mountain at the northernmost part of the country would be the first sentence and Hallasan, at the edge of the south, its last one. These two mountains are not only geographically similar in that they represent the beginning and end of the peninsula but of all the thousands of mountains Korea has, only these two have beautiful volcanic lake at the top. And they are also the highest mountains of North and South Korea respectively. By looking at the mountains appearance we can see that both Baekdusan and Hallasan are the representative symbols of the beauty of the Korean Peninsula.

Because of this, Koreans use the beautiful slogan "from Baekdusan to Hallasan" when referring to the entire nation and the reunification of Korea. This slogan, in other words, means "the alpha and the omega". But the original meaning of this slogan is found in the oriental tradition of the harmony of *eum* and *yang*. If we generalize, Baekdusan is masculine and Hallasan is feminine. If Baekdusan is a masculine mountain that carries a superb beauty, Hallasan reminds us of a mother embracing the plateau. One world be the *eum* and the other *yang*. Koreans understand the world as a place with rules of the universe where *eum* and *yang* are in harmony and because of this Baekdusan and Hallasan are the symbols of our "homeland".

If we see Hallasan as just a mountain, we are letting something more important pass by

Oreum

Oreum or the volcanic parasitic cones are one of the sources of pride of Hallasan and the people of Jejudo Island. Oreum comes from the word "oreuda" (climb) and it means independent mountain or peak in the Jejudo Island dialect. Hallasan possesses 368 parasitic cones. This is the most for any country in the world. It has more than 100 more parasitic cones the island of Sicily, which is the second place to have the most parasitic cones in the world. These cones are spread evenly throughout the entire island centered on Hallasan. Hallasan controls all the parasitic cones and makes all of Jejudo Island its territory. As if they had given their word of loyalty, these cones are the messengers of independent beauty, taking care of Hallasan on one hand and cultivating their own charm on the other. There are various shapes and types of parasitic cones. Some are 1,810 meters tall while others are only 41 meters tall.

Oreum are legendary homes carrying countless tales. Also they are the source of the living of Jejudo Island residents. Residents grow cattle and horses and cultivate the local land. Oreums are a resting place for the soul. We can see small and tidy tombs here and there in the oreums. Last of all, oreums show us the typical stone culture of Jejudo Island. The stones surrounding the graves, the little Buddha figures guarding the front of the tomb, these are Jejudo Island's unique culture established on top of nature. Oreum are the source of the living, the home to the legends and stone culture, and an abode to dwell after death.

2

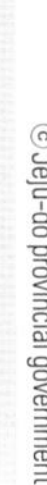
© Jeju-do provincial government

1. Tea fields and a scene of Mt. Hallasan's peak in the winter.
2. An aerial view of a oreum, parasitic cone, in Jejudo Island.
3. Baengnokdam, a beautiful lake found at Hallasan's mountaintop .
4. Roe deer and winter scenery of Mt. Hallasan.

3

ⓒ Jeju-do provincial government

4

ⓒ Jeju-do provincial government

5. Parasitic cones called Oreum.

without notice. This is because Hallasan is on Jejudo Island, the most beautiful island in northeast Asia. Venus and the clam are inseparable in Boticelli's "The Birth of Venus." Similarly, Hallasan and Jejudo Island are two inseparable things. Jejudo Island is a huge volcanic island. After an eruption in the Third Cenezoic Era, Hallasan shot up into the sky, and following the mountain range, Jejudo Island showed its true form. Later, big and small volcanic eruptions took place until 25,000 years ago. Consequently, a 1950 meters high mountain and a 1,820 square kilometers island was formed. Jejudo Island and Hallasan, both 88 miles away from the mainland, are two names for the same place. Hallasan is Jejudo Island and Jejudo Island is Hallasan.

The word Hallasan means "it can grab and pull a galaxy." This means that it is close to the sky and that it is as beautiful as a galaxy. Ever since humans started inhabiting Jejudo Island, Hallasan became the center of the habitat. Hunting, cattle-breeding, farming have all been based on Hallasan.

You can experience various climates in Hallasan. The mountaintop has an Arctic climate, the middle of the mountain a temperate climate and in the plains near the beach have a subtropical climate. Because of this, in Hallasan you can see a snow covered view and a tropical green area at the same time. Hallasan is a tourist site receving a worldwide spotlight because it is a blessed natural environment filled with curious and odd-looking stones, a high plateau and a volcanic lake at its

mountaintop. The name of the lake is Baengnokdam. In Korea it means "pond inhabited by white deer." In the old days, deer are said to have actually lived here, but now many roebucks, cousins to the deer, inhabit this lake.

If we measure importance by size, Hallasan is not an important mountain in the world. But because it is a treasure of rare plants, Hallasan's value is far from small. Hallasan grows more than 1,700 species of plants, 150 of which are considered worldwide rare species. Hallasan is a paradise of wild orchids. There are around 90 species of wild orchids of which 40 are rare species that are only grown in Jejudo Island. Natural Monument No. 191, the Cymbidium Orchid of Jejudo shows off its elegant and firm posture. Another attraction of this mountain is an old Korean(*Abies Koreana*) tree. This tree is said to live 1,000 years, die and then go on to live 1,000 years more.

The haggard and thin dead old tree left with only white branches hanging have found their places in the high plateau, look like a wise master or an abstract work of art.

Independent islands such as Tasmania have become a paradise of rare animals and plants by isolating the island from humans. Similarly, Jejudo Island has long maintained a biological isolation state from the mainland and hence possesses many valuable plants that support Darwin's theory. The Korean government and Jeju-do provincial government both very well know the value of this mountain and are gradually increasing the budget for its protection.

Fantastic golf courses

At the edge of Mt. Hallasan you can find many fantastic golf clubs. Many golf lovers around the world are enchanted with Jejudo Island golf courses, because you can view the ocean while you play in almost all the golf courses. The Ora Country Club is a popular Jejudo golf club with 36 holes. The Nine Bridge Country Club has 120 bunkers where you can fully enjoy this fascinating game. It is an excellent golf course enough to be included in the 100 best golf courses in the world. Golfers all agree that they stand in the teeing ground, they all feel a challenging spirit rising inside of them.
The Pinx Golf Club is as beautiful as the Nine Bridge Country Club. Ted Robinson, a world famous American golf course designer, designed this golf course. International competitions such as the LPGA World Championship are held in both these golf clubs very often. The hotel located inside the Pinx Golf Club is also famous. Because it looks like a bunch of grapes when you look down at it from the sky, it is called the "Grape Hotel."
The Jeju Country Club is north of Mt. Hallasan, standing at the high altitude of 560 meters above sea level and the Jeju Dynasty Country Club, at the foot of the mountain facting southeast, has a spectacular view of the ocean.

6. A scene of Nine Bridge Country Club in the middle of Mt. Hallasan.
7. Munjuran(Crinum asiaticum bar, japonica baker), Mt. Hallasan's native flower.

1

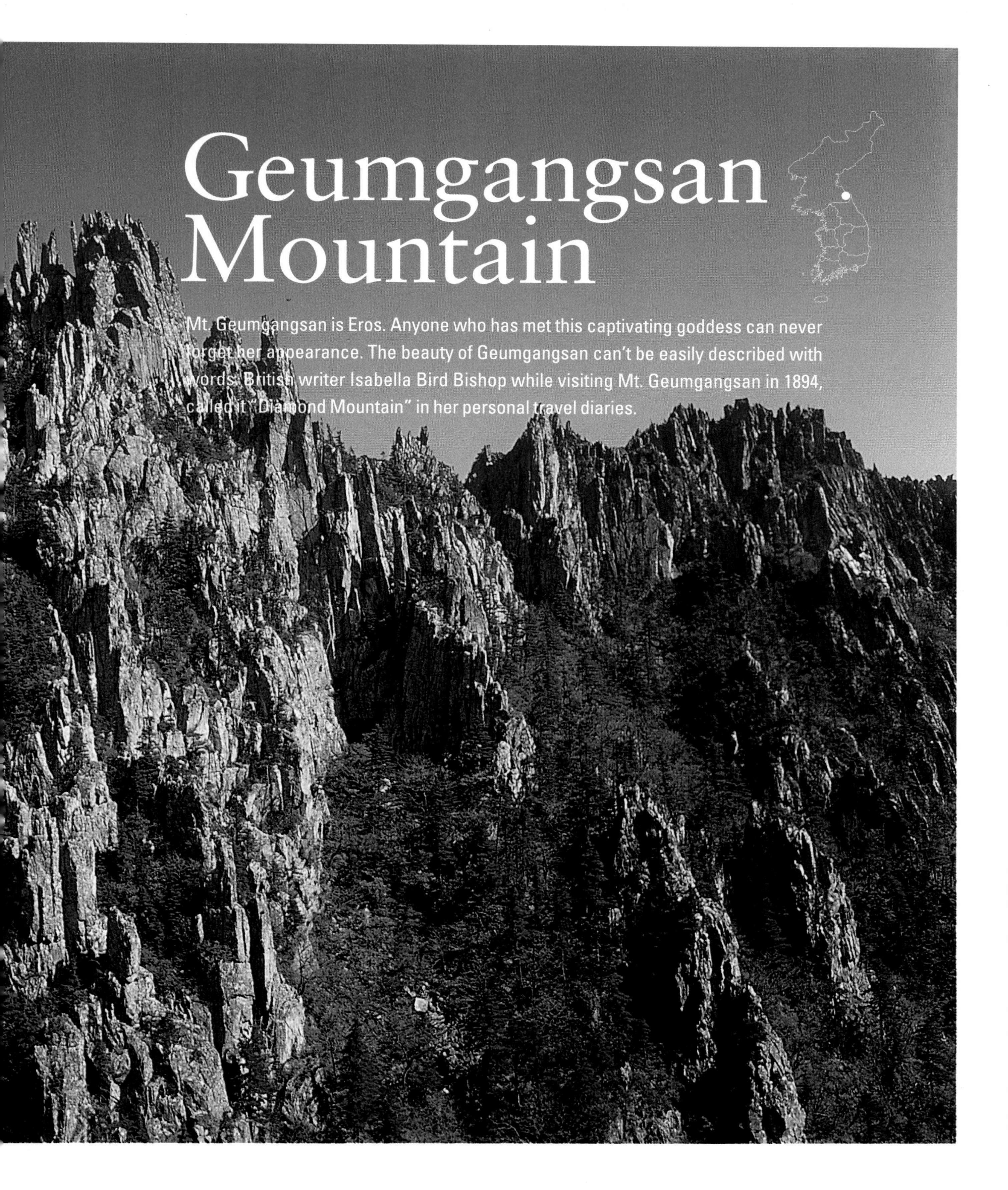

Geumgangsan Mountain

Mt. Geumgangsan is Eros. Anyone who has met this captivating goddess can never forget her appearance. The beauty of Geumgangsan can't be easily described with words. British writer Isabella Bird Bishop while visiting Mt. Geumgangsan in 1894, called it "Diamond Mountain" in her personal travel diaries.

1. Mt. Geumgangsan's stores.
2. Bongnaejeondo, painted by Jeong Seon (1676-1759), 130cm × 94cm, Leeum Museum.
3-4. Fall and summer scenery of Mt. Geumgangsan.
5. Snow covered Mt. Geumgangsan.

Mt. Geumgangsan is like Eros. Anyone who has met this captivating goddess can't forget her appearance. This lethal beauty that the Creator has left us excites all people. This is not just a modern day tale because traveling has become common. Even before the middle ages, Geumgangsan was a muse to Koreans. Every poet or painter had visited Geumgangsan during the Joseon Dynasty. This is because no one could speak with confidence about the beauty of nature without exploring Geumgangsan. Many dedications and praises of this mountain's beauty have left us with the best literature of the present day.

Besides this, the will of painters to paint Geumgangsan has been the motivation and strength that drove and lead the rapid development of Korean paintings. Among these, the late Joseon Dynasty's "Jingyeongsansuhwa", which has been acknowledged a peerless genre of oriental paintings, can be considered an artistic trend created by Geumgangsan without exaggeration. We have been able to confirm this through a great painter called Jeong Seon. As the Mediterranean sun inspired Picasso, so did the colors and geographical features of Geumgangsan inspire Jeong Seon. Jeong Seon's picture of Geumgangsan is an immortal masterpiece standing at the zenith of Joseon's art history. The captivating beauty of Geumgangsan can't be easily described with words. As an example, there is a Korean saying that goes, "Even Geumgangsan is a sight to see after a meal," meaning that even the beautiful Geumgansan must be seen after having a hearty meal to be properly appreciated. The message of this saying is trying to convey that the basic necessities comes before leisure. But why did they choose Geumgangsan? We may interpret the apparent paradox as an expression of how beautiful and charming these mountains are, at least almost enough to make to forget to eat a meal.

Let us look at another example. The admiration that Koreans felt for Geumgangsan was eventually interrupted due to the ceasefire line, the last gift given to South Koreans during the Cold War. After the Korean War in 1950, the 155-mile long barbed wired fence in the ceasefire line was stronger than any curtain in the world. But even though the South has occupied the vantage point in the rivalry between the two regimes, it has never refused to send financial aid to the North, a nation that has firmly supported socialism, in order to be permitted to travel to Geumgangsan. South Korea succeeded in becoming the 12th

A Korean fable - The Nymph and the Woodcutter

Geumgangsan's valleys and rocks each has its own fable. One of them is about a nymph and a woodcutter and related to a pond called Sangpaldam.

Once upon a time, there was an unmarried woodcutter who lived in a gorge. One day, the woodcutter saved and helped hide a fawn escaping some hunters. In return, the fawn let the woodcutter know a secret. On full moon days, nymphs came down from heaven and bathed in Sangpaldam. The fawn told the woodcutter that if he hid one of the nymph's wings while they were bathing, he could marry the one who wasn't able to fly. The woodcutter did as he was told, married the beautiful nymph, had three children and lived happily. But his wife missed the heavens very much. Taking pity on her, the woodcutter relented and told her the truth about that day (which he should have kept secret) and returned the wings to her. The wife took all three children and flew up to heaven leaving the woodcutter in grief and sadness. At this moment, the fawn came back and said that a well-bucket comes down from the heavens during full moon days to gather water and that if he was able to get on this well-bucket, he could go up to the heavens. Doing as he was told, the woodcutter went up to heaven, reunited with his wife and lived happily ever after. Sangpaldam is still as beautiful and clean as if nymphs came down to bathe in it.

© Hyundai Asan

© Hyundai Asan

6

economic power in the world in just 50 years from being one of the poorest country in the world.

A tourist route by ship to Geumgangsan started operation in 1997, and finally in 2003 a land route was open. With this, the barbed wire fence, which had been the symbol of the division between the South and North, was torn down. Nobel Peace laureate and former president Kim Dae-jung made an enormous effort to make this happen. This small and beautiful gap would have been impossible if not for Geumgangsan. The South and North leaned toward reconciliation by giving political responsibilites the non-political Geumgangsan. In other words, Geumgangsan's beauty literally tore down the barrier of different idelogies.

This mountain has been blessed with a climate that gives it four very different seasons.

7

© Hyundai Asan

Geumgangsan Tourist Guide for foreigners

Foreigners can also visit Geumgangsan. Just fill in a tourist application form for Geumgangsan, a recent photo (size 3.5cm × 4.5cm), and a copy of your passport. Without any other special conditions, your documents will certainly be accepted.

Don't forget that you should apply for this sightseeing tour at least 20 days prior to the departure date. You can pay for the trip with your credit card.

There are three types of sightseeing tours to Geumgangsan: half day tour, one day tour or two day tour. Independent sightseeing trips are not permitted. The itinerary is arranged and accomodated by the travel agency. You can choose from five different types of accommodations. Haegeumgang Hotel, a water-floating hotel, have the best facilities while the Hot Springs Village, a bungalow in the middle of a forest, has a romantic atmosphere while being a budget environmentally-friendly accommodation. Besides Geumgangsan climbing you can watch North Korean circus performance, one of the best circus performances in the world or dip in the hot springs of Onjeong, which has one of the best quality waters in the world. It also has excellent restaurants and shopping facilities. You can only use US dollars within Geumgangsan and, although somewhat limited, you may use an international credit card. You must also carry your passport at all times during your trip.

6. Guryeong Waterfalls. This waterfall is 82 meters high.
7. Local restaurants found in Mt.Geumgangsan.
8. Fall scenery of Mt. Geumgangsan leaves turning into autumn tints.

Geumgangsan looks entirely different at every changing season. This is why this mountain is called different names for every season. In the fall it is called Pungaksan, and here 'Pung' means fallen leaves. In the winter it is called Geogolsan, meaning mountain that shows its bones. In the summer it is called Bongnaesan. In the spring, it is called Geumgangsan. This name comes from the word 'vajra' in Sanskrit which means "utopia in the celestial universe" of the Buddhist world. Visiting Geumgangsan in 1894, British writer Isabella Bird Bishop called it "Diamond Mountain" in her personal travel diaries.

Generally, Geumgangsan is divided into three sections: Outer Geumgang, Inner Geumgang, and Sea Geumgang. Outer Geumgang is the east side of the line centered on its highest peak Birobong (1638 m) and stretches from north to south. These peaks are filled with odd-shaped stones and beautiful valleys. Also Outer Geumgang is famous for its impressive Manmulsang, Ongnyudong, Guryeong Waterfalls and Cheonbuldong Valley.

Inner Geumgang is the Western part of Biro bong and has many temples with long histories, and like the Outer Geumgang, has many beautiful valleys and peaks. While the Outer Geumgang is splendid, the Inner Geumgang has a more humble and quiet appearance.

Lastly, the Sea Geumgang area is the vast section of the coastal area where the East Sea and Geumgangsan meet. This is a paradise on earth filled with beautiful lakes, pine trees, strange looking rocks and marine cliffs.

8

Seoraksan Mountain

Mt. Seoraksan stands at 1,708 meters above sea level and is the third highest mountain in Korea after Mt. Hallasan and Mt. Jirisan. Seoraksan's "seor" means 'snow' in Korean. Mt. Seoraksan is located at the waistline of the Korean Peninsula and lies adjacent to the East Sea coast. It is connected to Mt. Geumgangsan at the top and faces Mt. Odaesan in the south.

Mt. Seoraksan(1,708m) is located at the waistline of the Korean Peninsula and lies adjacent to the East Coast. It is connected to Mt. Geumgangsan at the top and faces Mt. Odaesan in the south. The long mountain range that starts in Baekdusan and stretches to the South Coast is called Baekdu daegan. A long with Mt. Geumgangsan, Mt. Seoraksan is considered to be the most beautiful mountain in this mountain range. Both these mountains are the epitome of the majestic beauty that can be expressed by a mountain.

Prior to the 20th century, Seoraksan was in second place, and remained hidden behind Geumgangsan's spotlight. The magnificent splendor of Geumgangsan drew hoards of visitors and the majestic grandeur of Seoraksan was ignored. There was a clear explanation for this: Geumgangsan was much more accessible than Seoraksan. Before the 19th century, Seoraksan was closed on all four sides by valleys, rivers, oceans and rugged mountains. So people were unable to visit it even if they wanted to. After the 1950s, thanks to road construction and technology development, tunnels and bridges were built and Seoraksan finally unveiled its mysterious beauty. Many people from South Korea then started visiting Seoraksan instead of Geumgangsan, the latter being inaccessible due to the DMZ. Seoraksan left a strong impression to its visitors that it was not second to Geumgansan. Seoraksan has beautiful and outstanding features, clear and clean valleys, odd-shaped rock formations that make it a superb sight every season. As time goes by, you can discover new attractive aspects of Seoraksan and every year millions of visitors come to see it.

Seoraksan is the third highest mountain in Korea after Mt. Hallasan and Mt. Jirisan. Seoraksan's "seor" means 'snow' in Korean. It was given this name because it is covered with snow five months a year. The snow covered view of Seoraksan during the winter is simply breathtaking. If you look at the snow-covered landscape you will fell exhilirated. Seoraksan is was designated a National Park in 1970 and

after being recognized for its valuable and well-preserved ecological system it was chosen as a Biological Reserve Area by UNESCO in 1981. Generally, the eastern part of Seoraksan is called Oe(Outer) Seorak and the Western part Nae(Inner) Seorak. Nae Seorak faces the west, lies connected to the inland and its water stream is connected to the Hangang River. Oe Seorak crosses Sokcho and immediately flows to the sea. The most famous destination in Nae Seorak is Baekdam Valley, which means "valley with 100 ponds" in Korean. The scenic view of Seoraksan while standing on the ridgeline where this valley commences is awe-inspiring. At the downstream of the valley stands the historic Baekdamsa, the temple built during the Silla Kingdom, which became famous during the Japanese Ruling Era when a famous Buddhist monk, poet and thinker named Han Yongun stayed there to write.

Oe Seorak has a magnificent look with its mysterious rock formations. The 950 meter

1. Snow covered Baekdamsa Temple in Mt. Seoraksan.
2. Fall scenery of Mt. Seoraksan Valley with leaves turning into autumn tints.
3. Beautiful and bizarre rock formations found in Mt. Seoraksan

3

high vertically standing Ulsanam Rock is proof of this. The most prominent valley of Oe Seorak is the 15 kilometer long Cheonbuldong Valley. In the spring flower blossoms fill the mountain, in summer everything is dressed in green, in fall the trees are dyed of red and yellow and in winter magnificent snow-covered landscapes. In every season, Mother Nature invites every hill to a feast filling up the entire valley. There is probably no other mountain in Korea that can reproduce Vivaldi's Four Seasons as well as this mountain can. Taking a look at the names given to Seoraksan's peaks, valleys and rocks will greatly help visitors to appreciate this mountain. First of all, "Yongajangseong", one of the many ridgelines was given this name because it resembles the teeth of a dragon. The thickly-set, fang-like, sharp and pointy peaks look very mystical.

4. Fall scenery of Seoraksan Valley.

"Guimyeonam" means "devil face rock." It was given such a name because it has the grotesque shape of a standing person. "Chil-hyeongjebong" are seven rocks that were named thus after the tale of seven brothers who peeked at a nymph bathing in the valley and turned into stone. In the case of Geumgangsan, its charm is unrivaled. All the things that make up Geumgangsan show off their beauty. Like a woman with a beautiful countenance that can make you lose your mind. On the other hand, the charming point of Seoraksan is harmony. Each element in Seoraksan shows off its beauty. They all look at each other's face and form a harmonious group. That's why a trip to Seoraksan makes you feel not only lighthearted but comfortable and relaxed. Both these mountains are fraternal twins: they both have similar features and yet possess different charms.

5. Mt. Seoraksan has the perfect conditions to go ice climbing.
6. Mt. Odaesan at a distance.
7. Mt. Jirisan royal azalea blossoms.

Other mountains

1. Mt. Odaesan. Mt. Odaesan (1,563m) is located south of Mt. Seoraksan, at the southern part of the Baekdu daegan range. Odaesan means "five great peaks" in Korean. Many poets and scholars called this mountain generous and virtuous. This is true, because it is actually not very rough but has soft ridgelines compared to Geumgangsan or Seoraksan. In the religious world, Odaesan is a sacred place for Buddhists. In historic temples such as Woljeongsa and Sangwonsa, visitors can find proof of the close relation between Odaesan and Buddhism.

2. Mt. Deogyusan. Geographically, it is located almost at the center of South Korea . A famous destination in Mt. Deogyusan (1,594m) is the valley that originates from its peak and stretches more than 25 kilometer called Mujugucheondong. At the edge of Deogyusan is the largest ski resort in Korea. Based on this, the citizens of Muju are trying to host the next Winter Olympics.

3. Mt. Jirisan(1,915m). At the top of Mt. Jirisan stands a stone monument. The words written in this stone monument are "The spirit of Koreans originates here." All that can be seen around from it's peak are mountains. Thickly overlapping ridgelines are connected to the north to Deogyusan. To the south is a view of many islands several kilometers off the South Sea. There is no other place in Korea where one can appreciate the majestic scenery of the entire country except in Jirisan. It is not an exaggeration to say that patriotic love for Korea and growing sense of pride for being Korean springs forth in the hearts of those who climb Mt. Jirisan.

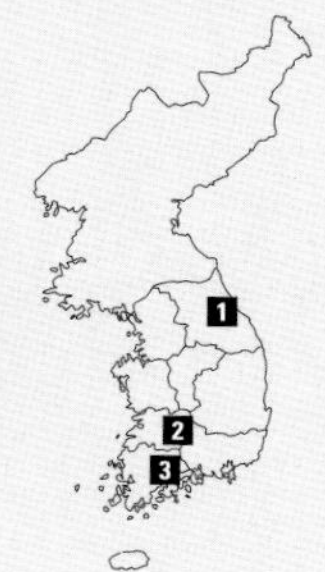

The East Sea

In the old times, Koreans believed there was a dragon king living in the East Sea. They believed that a kingdom of gods lived beyond the horizon in the vast and big ocean keeping all mysteries. This is why Koreans have special feelings toward the East Sea much like Mt. Baekdusan.

2

The East Sea is located at the east side of the Korean Peninsula. It is connected to the Sea of Okhotsk in the north, the Japanese archipelagos to the east, the Korea Strait in the south and faces the Pacific Ocean. It is a deep and blue sea that is 1,700 kilometers long (north to south) and 1,100 kilometers wide (east to west) and has an average depth of 1,361meters while in some places it is as deep as 4,049 meters. The coastal line is simple and if you go just a few meters into the ocean the depth of the water will become great. The East Sea is much more simple than the shallow and quiet West Sea or the Yellow Sea and its many islands, but it is more magnificent.

The East Sea does not have as many islands as the Yellow or South Sea. In the vast East Sea, there are only two islands inhabited by humans: Ulleungdo and Dokdo Island. Ulleungdo Island is located in the blue East Sea, resembling a diamond stuck in a large jade tray. It is 137 km off the east side of the mainland. A total of 9,200 people inhabit the 7,255 square kilometers piece of land. An island created from volcanic activity during the Third Cenozoic Era, it has very beautiful sceneries. Because of this, more than 200,000 people visit this island annually.

Ulleungdo is the outpost for squid fishermen. The night sky of Ulleungdo's coast is almost as bright as day due to the squid fishermen boat's fish-luring lights. Dokdo, a small island with odd rock formations located 92 kilometers off the southwest of Ulleungdo, is the eastmost Korean territory. Currently, two citizens inhabit it, and there are Dokdo patrol guards on duty. Ulleungdo and Dokdo were incorporated into Korea in 512 when Silla's General Yi Sabu admitted both these islands into the Silla Kingdom. (57BC – 935AD).

The Taebaek Mountain Range's steep downhill road is abruptly brought to an end when it meets the East Sea and due to these natural features of the East Sea coast, farming fields are almost non-existent. For the people in the coastal area, the sea was something to be loved and revered since it was their sole means of survival. Because of these reasons, since prehistoric times when navigation skills were still premature and until the early 20th century, fishing in the East Sea was a continuous fight at the risk of one's life.

The East Sea has been receiving attention from marine industries around the world as a gold fishing ground. Since cold and warm currents meet, cods, pollacks, sauries and cuttlefish are abundant. When night falls in the East Sea, electric lamps from fishing boats light up the sea. Particularly the lights from the cuttlefish boats's decorate the nightscape of the East sea. At dawn, these boats return to the harbor making churning engine sounds. Sokcho, located at the middle of the Korean Peninsula and the foot of Mt. Seoraksan, and Jeodong Port located in Ulleungo, an island floating in the East Sea are both outposts for cuttlefish fisheries.

Whale hunting was a lucrative business that generously filled the pockets of the fishermen in the East Coast until the late 1980's. The history of whale hunting in the East Sea goes back to the prehistoric age. In the ancient drawings of Daegok-ri, Ulsan remain detailed descriptions of primitive whale hunters carved

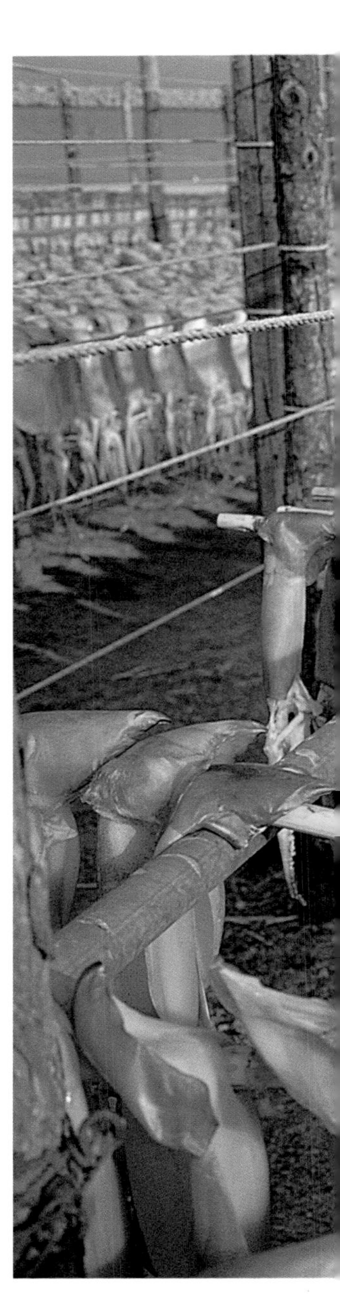

1. Ulleungdo, a volcanic island and Korea's eight largest island, found 137 kilometers off the East Coast.
2. Sunrise in Daewangam Rock, underwater tomb of King Munmu of the Silla Kingdom(57 BC-935 AD).
3. Women drying squid.

3

Cities of east coast belt

In the northern part of the East Coast the primitive and natural beauty is well-preserved. On the other hand, many large cities are in the southern part of coast where you can find both traces of the past and modern life in one place. On the edge of the south of the East Sea is Gyeongju, Silla Kingdom's 1,000 year-old capital city. The entire city of Gyeongju is a huge historical relic. Centered on Gyeongju, a triangle is formed with Pohang and Ulsan, and these three industrial cities formed the matrix of today's Korean economy. Pohang is a city that was formed after the POSCO was established there in 1970. Thirty years later, POSCO grew to become the most important steel maker in Asia and one of the five largest in the world. Ulsan, a city with the most important factories of the Hyundai conglomerate is an industrial city with the nickname Hyundai Republic. The Hyundai Motor factory was built in 1968 and the Hyundai Shipbuilding factory in 1973. Besides this, fertilizer, oil refining and chemicals companies are thickly-set in the east coast belt.

ⓒUlsan metroplotan city

by humans who lived there. Through these paintings, we know that whale hunting was done in the East Sea during the prehistoric age. These drawings are works of art of historical remains that very well demonstrate the lifestyle of the primitive hunting period and heart moving and touching images of fisherman fighting whales. Jangsaengpo, the outpost of whale fishing boat located in the present day Ulsan Metropolitan City was the most crowded and bustling port of the East Sea before the whale fishing prohibition treaty was implemented. The giant crabs caught in Yeongdeok, Gyeongsangbuk-do Province are

4. Fishermen out to catch king crabs.
5. View of Ulsan Metropolitan City.
6. Ulleungdo Island passenger ships and tourists.

high-class seafood sought after by epicures.

East Coast is a fair of lagoons. The gods must have taken pity while designing the rapid and simple East Sea coast and installed beautiful jewels along its coastline. These lagoons, formed by separating from the sea by a sandbar, are wonderful landscapes and have priceless ecological value. The elegance of the pine trees surrounding the lake is wonderful but more fantastic are the sight of the various migrating birds from Siberia that fly during the winter. Even now these lagoons are very well-preserved. Bordering on the ceasefire line are Gangdongho Lake, Hwajinpo Lake, Songjiho Lake, and Gyeongpoho Lake line from north to south.

Along with the lagoons, another sculpture from the gods in the East Sea coast are the rocky coastline. Various types of marine cliffs and marine plateaus have developed in this area, thanks to the coastline where the Baekdudaegan's steep peaks fall directly to the sea.

Mt. Geumgangsan, which is connected to Haegeumgang in Goseong-gun, Gangwon-do Province and Chongseokjeong in Tongcheon-gun and Chuam Beach of the East Sea are so beautiful they are all worth being called masterpieces of God.

7. Beautiful and bizarre rock formations, magnificent Chuam Beach in the East Sea.

The Yellow Sea

The west sea of Korea is internationally known as the Yellow Sea. Koreans often call it the Seohae (West Sea) because it is at west side of the peninsula. The Yellow Sea is located between China and Korea (east of China and west of Korea). It is a shallow sea only 41meters deep.

This sea is called the Yellow Sea because the large rivers dye the seawater a mud yellow color. China's Huanghe River and Yangtze River and Korea's Amnokgang, Daedonggang, Hangang and Geumgang Rivers all gather in the Yellow Sea. This is why the water is not very salty, it is abundant with plankton and is home to a varied marine fauna.

The shores at the west side of Korea are called Seohaean or West Coast. This coast starts in North Korea's Amnokgang River and reaches the Haenam Peninsula in the Jeollanam-do Province. The direct distance is 650 kilometer but because of the irregular coastline, the total distance of the coastal line is 4,700 kilometer. There are small and big ports along this coast, and more than 1,500 islands are in the nearby sea. Ganghwado and Anmyeondo are the two largest islands of the west coast and these are connected to the mainland by man-made bridges. The remaining islands are smaller and there are more deserted than inhabited islands. For example, Sinan-gun, at the Southwest of Jeollanam-do Province administrates 111 inhabited islands and 719 uninhabited islands. This is probably the largest number of islands administred by a local government in the world.

Since ancient times, the Yellow Sea has been widely used as a trading route connecting China, Korea and Japan. Through the Yellow Sea, the Baekje of Kingdom (18 BC–660 AD)managed to reach trading merchants in places as far as India and the Arabian Peninsula. Even now, international trade through the Yellow Sea is very active. The biggest and most important port in the west coast is Incheon. Incheon opened its port during the late 19th century and is also a historic city where US General Douglas MacArthur succeeded in his amphibious landing during the Korean War. Incheon, with its international trading port and the International Airport is a gateway to Korea. Mokpo

Byeonsan Peninsula National Park

The entire Byeonsan Peninsula of Buan-gun, Jeollabuk-do Province was named a National Park in 1988. The area of this park is 15,700ha and is surrounded by graceful mountains and seas. The Byeonsan Peninsula National Park is a beautiful place with small and large mountains, seas and islands, beaches, marine cliffs and historic temples.

The sedimentary rocks eroded from the seawater give it a look as it thousands of books piled up. The fine forest is very famous and the pinewood has been used since the Goryeo Dynasty as construction material for palaces. A place that cannot be left without mentioning in Byeonsan Peninsula is Naesosa, a 1,000 year-old temple. This temple is a treasure-level cultural heritage that possesses the famous Dongjong (bronze bell). And surrounding Daeungbojoen are fir trees that always leave visitors with a pure and clean feeling.

2

1. Aerial view of the Yellow Sea islands.
2. Naesosa Temple in the Byeonsan Peninsula, Jeollabuk-do province.
3. Octopus caught in tidelands.
4. A family playing with mud in tidelands.
5. Reed fields at the shores of Seocheon-gun, Chungcheongnam-do Province. Shooting location for the Korean film "JSA".

and Gunsan are the largest commercial ports of the peninsula's southern west coast.

However, the real attraction of the Korean West Coast is not these huge port cities. The heavily indented coastal line with countless small inlets shows the real attractive point of the West Coast. The small inlets show a tranquil scenery with seagulls resting on top of a few fishing boats inside the bulwark. Ships can be seen in even smaller inlets without bulwarks lying on tidelands where the seafloor is disclosed due to the low tides. If the moon didn't orbit around the earth, the West Coast tidelands would not exist. Over time, the countless high and low tides of the seawater in Seohaean (West Coast) have made it one of the five best tidelands in the world. These tidelands are an important watchdog that must exist for the normal cycle of the marine ecology. Tidelands are incubators for sea life and are also powerful cleaners that purify their own polluted sea. Tidelands have developed in almost every area of the west coast. The Korean Peninsula is highly elevated on the east and lower towards the West Coast, becoming almost a flatland. Because this flat area is directly connected to the sea strong high and low tides exist. In the West Coast, tens of hectares of tidelands appear and disappear every year.

Nature, the life of the people based on Seohaean and the tidelands are three inseparable elements. The tidelands say everything about the West Coast. The ports, the fishermen's lives and their culture have developed around the tidelands. Even now most of the West Coast area remains this way.

One example that shows how much attention the tidelands are getting in the West Coast is the Mud Festival. This festival is held in Boryeong, Chungcheongnam-do Province and is an event based on first-hand experience. Visitors do almost anything that can be done with mud. Mud pools, mud massages, mud facial masks and mud cosmetics. The tidelands of the West Coast are gifts from God that help nature and people.

6. Salt fields on the West Coast.
7. Anmyeondo island's pine tree forest.
8. A Sunset in the West Coast, reminding one of a traditional oriental painting.

Anmyeondo island

This is an island in Taean-gun, Chungcheongnam-do Province. It measures 5.5 kilometer east to west, 24 kilometers north to south and has area of 90 square kilometers. It is Korea's seventh largest island and has an around 10,000 inhabitants. This island has around 10 beaches and several ecologically priceless tidelands.

The most famous element in Anmyeondo is the pine forest. Pine trees that are over 100 years old are spread over an area of 4.3 square kilometers. This pine tree wood is of the highest quality and has been used to build palaces or ships since the Goryeo Dynasty. However, because of several thoughtless citizens who cut these pine trees and used it as firewood, the palace sent a government official to watch over them. This entire pine forest is a natural recreational forest. The International Flower Fair was held in 2002 here, and now a flower festival is held every year in spring. Recently Anmyeondo is garnering attention as an ecological tourist site. Cheonsuman Bay, located close to Anmyeondo, is the largest returning spot for migrant birds in Korea. During winter, millions of migrant birds visit this place. When these birds fly and flock together the sky becomes dark as if painted with dark ink.

8

The South Sea

The South Sea is located in the Southern region of the Korean Peninsula. It is such a breathtakingly beautiful place that almost every spot has been designated a National Park, and more than 2000 islands are scattered near its shorelines. This is why people call this sea "Dadohae," which in Korean means "sea with many islands."

Past the evergreen pine forest is a descending slope. The clear rocks lie in the ridgeline at the mountain at their front and later, an uphill mountain, you will meet an uphill mountain. At the foot of the mountain are affectionate densely-set furrows in the fields as well as sun rays reflected on the roofs of some scattered farm houses. The breeze is gentle and sweet. The car leaves the peaceful countryside behind and climbs uphill. Suddenly the full view of the jade-like green sea is at one's. An impressive panorama of the beautiful sea and green islands stuck like jewels unfolds infinitely in front of one's eyes. This is typical scene anyone can see in any part of the South Sea. While the East Sea is said to be masculine, the South Sea is agreeable, friendly and feminine. The South Sea survives by adapting to its environment rather than by challenging it. This sea is something that we must accept in our lives, beyond its beautiful scenery.

The South Sea is located in the southern region of the Korean Peninsula. Geographically, the coast of the South Sea extends from Mokpo port at the west to Busan port at the east, and the direct distance between these two ports is 250 kilometers. Because it is a heavily indented coastal area, the actual distance of this coast is over 8.8 times longer than the direct distance. It is such a breathtakingly beautiful area that almost every spot has been designated a National Park, and more than 200 islands are scattered near its shorelines. This is why people call this sea "Dadohae," which in Korean means "sea with many islands."

The South Sea is beautiful as well as abundant. Because its waters are warm they are perfect for fish spawning grounds, and is also good for fish and marine industry. Farming of marine products such as algae, fish and shellfish have developed well. Because the South Sea has better quality fish products than other seas in Korea, the fishermen enjoy a more plentiful and abundant life than in the East or Yellow Sea. Rarely shaped cliffs, white sandy shores, pine forests that hang like a folding screen decorate the winding coast, and along the coastal line small fishing villages can be spotted like commas in a graceful sentence.

Many notable Korean artists grew up here inspired, expanding their imagination with the beautiful surroundings. An interesting study about this area explains that during the Joseon Dynasty (1392–1910) many political criminals, mostly scholars, politicians, artists and philosophers were banished to islands in the South Sea, simply because these islands were the furthest away from Seoul. Much like stories in movies the exiles fell in love with native island women and gave birth to intelligent and gifted children. Of course, most of these talented offspring were not admitted into the mainstream society but started showing their abilities in the artistic field. Therefore, it is not a simple coincidence that after the feudal hierarchical society met its downfall in the early 20th century, talented people in every artistic area came forth from Tongyeong, Namhae-gun, Haenam-gun, Gangjin-gun and Bogildo Island (or the area dubbed the South Sea Belt).

There are two Marine National Parks in the

1. The South Sea islands seemingly floating in the ocean.
2. Fossils of dinosaur footsteps in the South Coast.
3. A beautiful view of Jindo Bridge. This bridge is located between Jindo and Haenam-gun in Jeollanam-do Province.

4

5

6

South Sea. They take up more than 80 percent of the coastal area. In 1968 Hallyeosudo Marine National Park, taking up more than half of the eastern part of the South Sea, was named a national park. The coastal area and islands that are included in this national park are as beautiful as a painting. Yeosu is a breathtaking port city surrounded by mountains and the South Sea. Sacheon, right next to the South Sea, is an important fishing port. In Goseong-gun at the east, you can find remaining prehistoric dolmens and fossilized dinosaur footsteps of the Cenozoic Era. Tongyeong, which has the most beautiful port in Korea, is a city of culture and art, and hometown to composer Yun Yisang and poet Kim Chunsu. Geojaedo Island, which is connected to Tongyeong by a bridge, has some bad past memories because it used to be a North Korean POW camp during the Korean War. At the same time it has the Okpo shipbuilding yard, home to a cluster of world-famous shipbuilding yards.

Dadohae Marine National Park, which takes up more than half of the west of the South East coast, was named so in 1981. The entire area is brimming with all types of islands. The scenery of the heavily indented coast and islands meeting and disappearing, repeatedly continues along the coastal roads. Islands such as Dolsando, Jindo, Wando and Bogildo found here, are similar to each other but have entirely different sceneries and atmospheres. Only visitors who open their hearts, and are attentive, can truly appreciate these charming islands.

4. Breathtaking view of Maemuldo Island, Tongyeong, Gyeongsang nam-do Province
5-6. Fisherman catching cutlass fish with fish-luring lights and cutlassfish.
7. Camellias with magnificent red colors. Numerous camellia tree forests are found in the South Sea Coast islands.
8-9. Picture of Geobukson (the Turtle Ship) and figure of Admiral Yi Sunsin.

Admiral Yi Sunsin

A special theme that well explains the South Sea is Admiral Yi Sunsin. The Imjin Waeran Wars, which started in 1592 and lasted for seven years, was an invasion led by Japan that left Joseon in ruins. Admiral Yi Sunsin, who commanded the Joseon naval forces, led all the sea battles into victory and turned the war into their favor. Yi Sunsin, the naval commander, commanded a revolutionary battleship called "Geobukseon" (or Turtle Ship) and commenced a sweeping counterattack.

Even though they were outnumbered, Yi Sunsin's battleship departed from Yeosu, and won one battle after another, and finally chased and destroyed (crushed) the Japanese navy warships in Busan and regained the South Sea. Numerous important and victorious sea battles have left their name in the world navy history books, and are currently being studied as success models in navy academies. Almost every coastal area between Yeosu and Busan is a victorious battleground for Admiral Yi Sunsin. Even now, there are several remains that commemorate him in the South Coast. Among these, Yeosu's Jinnamgwan (National Treasure No.304), the navy headquarter during the mid-Joseon Dynasty and Tongyeong's Saebyeonggwan (National Treasure No.305) are architecturally beautiful cultural heritages.

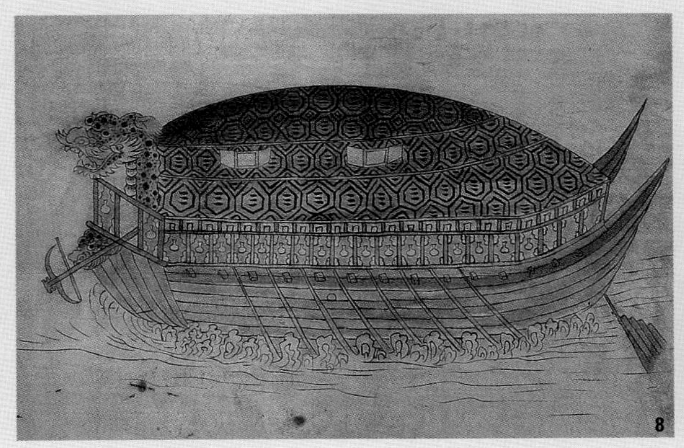

Jejudo Island

Jejudo is an island with beautiful natural settings and a unique traditional culture. Jejudo is the largest island located at the furthest south of Korea. Jejudo island is paradise in the North Pacific. The Newsweek magazine claimed Jejudo Island to be the "The Island of the Gods".

© Jeju-do provincial government

Jejudo Island is the largest island located at the furthest south of Korea. People inhabited Jejudo Island since the Neolithic Age. Since around BC 1 to 1000 AD it was governed under an independent nation system called "Tamna". This is why Jejudo Island is sometimes called Tamnado Island.

Jejudo Island is not only the most beautiful island in the Korean Peninsula, but of all northeast Asia. The volcanic activities during the Third Cenozoic Era produced a beautiful island on an important sea route in northeast Asia. This young volcanic island that was born millions of years ago has very unique geographical features and sceneries. This uniqueness can be observed at the aesthetic underground space it has left at the center of the island where five lava tubes have been discovered. These are intentionally left untouched, and many more are being preserved, to be used as tourist sites. Among these, Manjang Cave, and Ssangyeong Cave have a privileged post in the "world of caves." Manjang Cave, located at the East of Jejudo Island is 14,678 yards long, making it the longest lava tube in the world. The cave is internally filled with abstract works of art that no talented architect could ever imitate. In other words, the Creator's exhibition hall is open all year round.

At the west of Jejudo Island lies the smaller Ssangyong Cave. The name of this cave derives from the two dragons carved inside, who are said to have left their traces after passing through according to legends. It is an unmatching masterpiece of a mingled composition. The reason the phrase mingled composition is used is because this is the world's only cave made of lava that is also a limestone cave. It is a geologically unique cave that was made over an extensive period of time. The golden color of the cave was made when powder from clamshells filtered into the black lava and changed the color of the limestone cave. This cave is still evolving. On a hot summer day or a bitter cold winter day, the cave maintains a cool 15 °C. Along with Cachi Machay, Peru's stone salt cave and Cerjanska Pecina Serbia's underwater limestone cave, this cave is praised as one of the three best caves in the world.

The lava did not end its memorable magic show in the inland. The volcanic activity made its final curtain call by leaving breathtaking islands at the neighboring waters of Jejudo Island. Among these, Udo in the east, Biyangdo

1. Aerial view of Jejudo Island's Ilchulbong(sunrise atop a mountain peak).
2. Jejudo Island's native pony.
3. General view of Jungmun Resort Complex.
4. Jejudo Island's traditional thatched-roof houses and Mt. Sanbangsan, a volcanic cone

Jungmun Tourist Complex

This is world-level comprehensive tourist resort complex. All the famous resort hotels with the best facilities in Jejudo Island such as Shilla, Lotte and Hyatt Hotel are gathered here. You will find a botanical garden, where you can see diverse trees and flowers from around the world in one place along with an ocean aquarium, duty free shop, casino, golf course. All of these are located inside the hotels or in close proximity to them. There is also a beach at a walking distance from the hotel. If you walk along the hotel's promenade towards the ocean you will see the beach. In Jungmun, there is an international scale convention center where international events are held at all times. A five-minute walk away from the tourist complex will take you to the beautiful Cheonjeyeon Waterfalls. This waterfall, which means "nymphs from heavens bathing on the waterfall," is divided into three smaller parts: upper, middle and lower. Each waterfall is around 20 meters high. Rare plants live on both sides of the waterfall valley, and there is a dense subtropical forest, making it a very important ecological location.

4

Traditional life in Jejudo Island

Because Jejudo Island is separated from the mainland, it has always possessed a unique lifestyle and culture. In this island there are many places where Jejudo Island's unique way of life and culture can be experienced. Among these, the most representative is Seongeup Fok Village. This is a traditional village that shows the folk characteristics of Jejudo Island. The unique landscapes and island village's native primitive images are well preserved. Tangible and intangible cultural heritages such as the dolharubang, millstones worked by a horse or ox, places where palaces used to exist, folk games, local foods, folk art and crafts and the Jejudo dialect can be seen everywhere in the village. Because these people are actually living there, one can vividly feel and experience how the old inhabitants of Jejudo Island lived in ancient times. The Jejudo Folk Village Museum located in Pyoseon-myeon, Namjeju-gun, is the perfect place to glance at the Jejudo Islander's way of life. One can observe the at the characteristics of Jeju's diverse homes, for instance, the appearance and structure of dwellings at the seashore or mountains, homes of yangban and government office buildings and how these were different from each another. One can also discover how residents cultivated their land and how they fished. Besides this, visit the Jeju Folk Natural History Museum and the Jeju Folk Museum are wonderful places to see Jejudo's natural, lifestyle and cultural history at a glance.

5

6

in the west, Chujado in the North, Marado in the south are four that would win prizes in an island beauty contest. Particularly Marado is a special island because it is the island located at the southernmost end of Korea.

Now let's take a detailed look into this island. The fact that Jejudo Island is an isolated place in the middle of the sea has helped foster rare animals and plants everywhere in the island. Currently many rare creatures are living in Jejudo Island and these speak volumes on the diverse environments of the earth. The entire island of Jejudo is a prospective candidate for the UNESCO Natural Heritages.

The countless parasitic cones, worldwide known lava caves, diverse rare plants and animals are all part of the precious nature humans must protect. If the tour guide takes visitors to ride horses in Jejudo Island, remember that the ancestors of these horses probably came from Mongolia. The history of horse breeding in Jejudo Island goes back 1,000 years to Mongolia, that set up a local enterprise that managed the ranch and supplied horses to Jejudo Island during the Goryeo Dynasty. The fact that Jejudo Island has the perfect climate and land for breeding horses signifies that it is also good for people to live in. Jejudo Island is said to have three things that other places do not have: Wind, stones and women. Because of this, Jejudo Island is sometimes called "Samdado" which means "island with three plenties". The fact that it has more wind is not helpful in farming. However, the ancient people of Jejudo came up with an ingenious idea. When clearing the farming fields, the farmers used the basalt from the earth and made a waist high barrier that protected the crops. Without their wise plan to expand their fields and protecting the fields at the same time, the rest of the country could not enjoy Jejudo indigenous products such as carrots or tangerines. The stone barriers were used not only to protect crops but also to protect their homes. The reason why in the past more women live in this island is because many men died while fishing in the sea. The people of Jeju earned their living from the sea but lost many men to it as well. This seemingly happy beautiful island ironically possesses many sad memories.

5. Snow covered view of Jeju Folk Village Museum in Pyoseon-myeon.
6. Magnificent view of Seogwipo Port.
7. Rape flowers and Parasitic cones called Oreum.
8. Haenyeo, women divers, with nets filled with abalone and turban shells.

Cultural Heritages

Dolmen

The dolmen is one of the most representative historic characteristics that helps explain the Bronze Age. Around 30,000 dolmen are spread all over the Korean Peninsula. The Korean dolmens are a World Heritage.

Goindol(Dolmen) pertains to a type of megalithic culture. Dolmens are widely spread throughout Europe and Asia but most of them can be found in the Korean Peninsula. Around 30,000 dolmen are spread all over the peninsula. The dolmen is one of the most prominent historic characteristics that helps explain the Bronze Age. The dolmen contains shamanism and religious meanings. Dolmen are very valuable material and their preservation is imperative since they allow us to understand the prehistoric cultural lifestyle, their social and political structure as well as their beliefs and spiritual world.

The Korean dolmens are Bronze Age cultural heritages that are as excellent as the Egyptian pyramids, obelisks or Stonehenge. They show the spiritual world and the way of life of the people who worshiped these large stones. Although dolmens spread evenly spread throughout most of the world, they are mainly found densely clustered in northeast Asia, and among these areas, Korea has the largest distribution in the world.

Goindol in Korean means, "raised with three or four collected stone slabs". Although these dolmens were used as gathering places, rite altars, cemetery tombstones, they were mostly used as graves.

How were the prehistoric humans able to move these enormous stones? We can think about the flipside of these huge prehistoric stones. The prehistoric age was not a time of science and technology development. Therefore it is only logical that many people must have participated in carrying these big stones. If we imagine these people carrying the

1. Table type dolmen found in Ganghwado Island, Incheon.
2. Go-board type dolmen found in Gochang, Jeollabuk-do Province.
3. Go-board type dolmen found in Goheung, Jeollanam-do Province
4. Cluster of dolmens found in Gochang, Jeollabuk-do Province.

4

5

stones we can get a sense of the power of the authority that controlled and made them participate in moving the stones.

At the time these dolmens were made, there was a hierarchical system existing in the Korean society. And these powerful authorities had enough power to order crowds of people to make their tombs after they died. The higher the rank, the larger and taller the stones were.

The dolmens can be generally divided into northern type, southern type and the 'capstone' dolmens. The northern dolmen is also called 'table type' dolmen because it is an above-ground construction where a burial chamber is built on the ground, four stone slabs are set on it, and a large capstone is laid on top. On the other hand, the southern type is called the 'go-board type' because the burial chamber is constructed below the ground, and later the capstone is supported on a number of stones laid on the ground. The so-called 'capstone' type is a variant of the go-board type in which the capstone is laid directly on the buried slabs.

Many relics have been excavated from Korean dolmen, mainly stone daggers, stone and bronze arrowheads, bronze axes and deco-

6

Three prehistoric dolmen sites

In Gochang, Jeollabuk-do Province exists the most representative dolmen museum. In Jungnim-ri, Asan-myeon Gochang-gun you can find a group of 442 dolmens in an area of 57.22 hectares. The dolmens in Gochang are apparently a tribal group's family grave that used to govern the local region. In this region, you can see all three types of dolmens in one place. The types of dolmens are the northern 'table' type, the southern 'go-board' type and the capstone type. Dolmen of all sizes are found, the smallest weighing 10 tons and the largest weighing up to 300 tons.

The dolmen sites in Hwasun, Jeollanam-do Province have recently discovered and are in good state of preservation. There are around 500 southern type dolmens in Hyosan-ri, Dogok-myeon, and Daesin-ri, Chunyang-myeon. Along with dolmens, various relics have been found such as stone, earth and bronze artifacts and personal ornaments in tombs made of stone, ceramic jar, stone wall and wood. Also close to the prehistoric sites, you will find a stone gathering ground that shows the dolmen's construction process. This is a place where you can take a look at how the prehistoric people handled the stones, how they made the dolmens and carried them.

The Ganghwa, Incheon dolmen sites are at a high altitude of 100 meters to 200 meters above sea level, which is higher than the average altitude. Here you will find the largest northern type dolmen, whose capstone is 7.1 meters long and 2.6 meters tall.

rative accessories. Among these, the bronze mandolin sword, which is an item used only a special group in the Bronze Age society is the by ancient relic most Koreans are proud of.

There are 30,000 dolmens spread throughout Korea. However, the dolmens in the Gochang, Hwasun, Ganghwa archeological areas have a concentrated and great variety of dolmens that cannot be seen in other countries. The dolmens in these areas vividly show their development of technology and the social situation in the prehistoric age, and this has been recognized for their high value and designated a World Heritage by UNESCO. These dolmens are graves and funeral ceremony memorials made 2,000-3,000 years ago that let us know the lives and spiritual world of the prehistoric humans.

The prehistoric humans believed that stones were eternal, which is why they chose stones as their dwelling after death. So even though they died, they raised dolmens to live forever. And as they desired, after a long time trespassed, these stones are still guarding their place. Thanks to these many stones, Korea has become a “dolmen nation”.

5. Cluster of go-board type dolmens.
6. Table type dolmen found in Hwasun, Jeollanam-do Province.
7. Table type dolmen found in Gochang, Jeollabuk-do Province.

Buddhism

Buddhism was introduced to Korea around the 4th or 5th century. As Buddhism was introduced to Korea, more and more temples slowly started appearing in these Peninsula. After building the temples, people made diverse Buddha figures, built pagodas and carved Buddhist scriptures. Consequently, Korean architecture and art grew its roots along with Buddhism. Buddhism and Buddhist culture has surpassed the realm of religion, and has become a cultural heritage and an essential part of Korean history.

© Lee Gabchul

2

Buddhism in Korea

Buddhism was introduced to Korea around the 4th or 5th century. Prior to this, Koreans relied on Shamanism for their physical and spiritual lives. However, the leaders of the ancient kingdom felt the need for a stronger religion than Shamanism that could unify the entire nation. Goguryeo and Baekje adopted Buddhism directly from China while Silla adopted it from Goguryeo. The Koreans who accepted this Buddhist culture, combined it appropriately with their own native culture and made a new, superior ethnic culture. They also passed this culture on to Japan, and helped develop the foundation for Japan's primitive civilizations.

As Buddhism came into Korea, more and more temples slowly started appearing in the Peninsula. Most of the temples face the south. In fact, most of the Korean architecture is built to face south including buildings and even graves. This is because the homes can receive a lot of sunshine and warm breeze if they face south. After building the temples, people made diverse Buddha figures, built pagodas and carved Buddhist scriptures. Consequently, Korean architecture and art grew its roots along with Buddhism. Buddhism and Buddhist culture has surpassed the realm of religion, but is a cultural heritage and a part of the Korean history.

There are countless temples in Korea that are more than a 1,000 years old. Most of these temples are hidden in mountains. When Buddhism was first introduced to Korea, they were built in flat plains around the capital city, but as time went by, they gradually went up the mountains. The first Korean Buddhism was a political ideology used to govern a nation, a means to educate the common people and a religion that wished for people's happiness and wealth. However, as time went by, Buddhism changed into a variety of forms. One of them is Seonjong or Zen Buddhism. Seonjong survived the Goryeo Dynasty (918–1392). Seonjong was not focused on educating the people or on political ideologies but concentrated on teaching people to let go of their worldly desires and achieve enlightenment. Since mountains are peaceful and not crowded, they made the perfect place for Buddhist monks to study the Buddhist scriptures and do Zen meditation. Even now, Seonjong is the center of Korean Buddhist culture.

Bulguksa Temple, the house of Buddha

In 751 AD, the Silla citizens started to build Bulguksa Temple at the foot of Mt. Tohamsan as a fervent wish to realize Buddha's ideal nation in the real world. This is a rarely-seen Buddhist masterpiece that allows you to see architectural, geometrical and mathematical skills working together. Buddhist orderliness and ideals are reflected upon the design and architecture of the structure and arrangement of the temple.

Bulguksa can be divided into three areas: Daeungjeon Hall, Geungnakjeon Hall and Birojeon Hall. Each of these stands for the ideal lands in Buddhism. Daeungjeon refers to Sakyamuni or Buddha's land, Geungnakjeon signifies the Amitabha's paradise land and Birojeon stands for Buddha Birojana's (Vairocana) land of Truth.

1. A Buddhist monk of Haeinsa Temple in Hapcheon.
2. A complete aerial view of Bulguksa Temple.
3. Bulguksa Temple as seen from its entrance. The arch-shaped bridge at the middle of the stairs is Cheongungyo(blue cloud) Bridge. The one seen from the second floor stairs is Baegungyo(white cloud) Bridge.

3

If you enter Daeungjeon you must cross the Cheongungyo and Baegungyo Bridges. Cheongungyo and Baegungyo stand for "blue and white cloud bridges." Cossing these bridges, you are leaving the world behind, crossing the blue and white clouds, and entering the heavenly land of Buddha. Similarly, to enter Geungnakjeon, you must cross the Yeonhwagyo (Lotus Flower Bridge) and Chilbogyo (Seven Treasure Bridge). The steps on the stairway of Yeonhwagyo have beautiful patterns of lotus flowers carvings. All four bridges have been designated national treasures.

There are two pagodas in front of Daeungjeon. First, Seokgatap (National Treasure No. 21) or "pagoda of Buddha" expresses the beauty of the spiritual world that can be seen only through our hearts. The second one is Dabotap (National Treasure No. 20), showing the splendor of the material world. Both these pagodas show the harmony and balance between the human's material and spiritual world. Soekgatap shows the typical 3-story stone pagoda. This stone pagoda is an 8th century cultural masterpiece with its minimal decoration and balanced proportions. In 1966, during restorations done to Seokgatap, the world's oldest wooden printing blocks (National Treasure No. 126) were found inside the sari box. Dabotap takes after the traditional four-angle tile houses. This pagoda has a splendor and unique quality that is unseen in other pagodas and has completely broken off from the general standards of stone pagodas architecture. The idea for its creation is extraordinarily clever and original. They are also uncommonly beautiful. Architecturally, Bulguksa is a structure that brilliantly harmonizes stones and wood. The bridges and pagoda itself are made of stone and the remaining wood structures compose the entire beautiful Bulguksa, while each maintains its own individuality and independence.

Three Treasures (Sambo) Temples

Sambo refers to the three types of treasures in Buddhism. The three treasures are Buddha,

4. A Buddhist monk doing Zen meditation.
5. Muryangsujeon Hall in Buseoksa Temple is an 800-years old wood structure. National Treasure No. 18.
6. The participants in a Buddhist retreat take a walk around the temple and offer early morning prayers.

Temple architecture

Korean temples are exhibition halls of wooden architectures. Among these, Bongjeongsa, Buseoksa and Sudeoksa Temples are architectural museums that house the oldest temples in Korea. These three temples are beautiful wooden structures that were built 700–800. Bongjeongsa is the most notable temple of Andong, Gyeongsangbuk-do Province. Built in 682, this temple contains a wooden structure that is more than 800 years old. The name of that structure is Geungnakjeon Hall (National Treasure No. 15). This is the oldest wooden structure in Korea and has great cultural value in the history of Korean architecture. In April 1999, British Queen Elizabeth II only visited this temple. She said of Geungnakjeon, "it is a humble and modest but refined structure."

Buseoksa temple is in the Yeongju, Gyeongsangbuk-do Province, there is a very old temple built in 676. Buseoksa means "temple of the floating stone" in Korean. Its main hall called Muryangsujeon Hall(National Treasure No. 18) is Buseoksa's face. Scholars estimate that Muryangsujeon was built around the mid or late 1200s. Muryangsujeon is a masterpiece demonstrating the mature architectural beauty of the Goryeo Dynasty.

Sudeoksa is a temple built in Mt. Deoksungsan, Yesan, Chungcheongnam-do Province. The highlight of Sudeoksa is its main hall or Daeungjeon Hall(National Treasure No. 49). Built in 1307, it is around 700 years old. The Daeungjeon in Sudeoksa is more majestic and masculine than the above mentioned Geungnakjeon in Bongjongsa and Muryangsujeon in Buseoksa. In addition, its proportional balance is absolutely flawless.

6

Buddhist scriptures and great Buddhist monks. The three temples that have one of these treasures are called Sambo (three treasures) temples. These temples are Tongdosa, Haeinsa, and Songgwangsa. Tongdosa Temple have the sarira of the Sukyamuni Buddha, Haeinsa Temple holds a complete copy of the Tripitaka Koreana, and the collected writings of Mahayana Buddhism, the Songgwangsa Temple has produced 16 great Buddhist monks who have endlessly practiced the teachings of Buddha.

Tongdosa is in Yangsan Gyeongsangnam-do Province. As soon as he came back from Tang, China, a monk from the Silla period(57 BC–935 AD) called Jajang yulsa built Tongdosa with the garments he was wearing and relics from the Buddha himself. In the Daeungjeon (main building) of Tongdosa temple, you cannot see any statues of Buddha around the temple. This is because this temple houses the remnants of Buddha himself and a statue of Buddha was thought to be unnecessary.

Haeinsa is a temple located in a beautiful mountain called Gayasan at Hapcheon, Gyeongsangnam-do Province. Haeinsa is one of the most important temples in Korea because it houses the Tripitaka Koreana. Around 800 years ago, the people of Goryeo(918–1392) carved 80,000 wood-blocks for 16 years in order to organize and arrange the precious words of Buddha. This was made as an act of faith intended to bring the intervention of Buddha to Korea's cause during the invasion of the Mongols.

The Tripitaka Koreana houses rare and accurate documents that do not contain a single error. Japan's Buddhist scriptures and other nation's Buddhist Scriptures were made based on this Tripitaka Koreana. The Tripitaka Koreana is now kept in a building called Janggyeong Panjeon Hall in Haeinsa Temple. This structure was so scientifically made that for 800 years, not a single wooden block has been damaged. In 1995, recognized for their cultural and scientific value, both the Tripitaka Koreana and Janggyeong Panjeon were added to the UNESCO World Heritage list.

The historic Songgwangsa Temple is located at the foot of Mt. Jogyesan in Suncheon, Jeollanam-do Province. The ancient rulers of Korea gave virtuous and learned monks the title of 'guksa', which means "monk of the nation." Songgwangsa Temple, which was built during the latter years of the Silla Kingdom, has produced 16 guksa during 180 years, since the mid-Goryeo period to early Joseon period (1392–1910). If you visit the Guksajeon Hall of Songgwangsa Temple, you can see the enshrined portraits of these famous 16 Buddhist masters. A look at Guksajeon Hall will allow a deep understanding of the spirit and tradition of Songgwangsa Temple.

Stupas

The word Korean word for pagoda or 'tap' originated from the Hindustani word "stupa". These are "houses of spirits" where the sari of Buddha or virtuous and great Buddhist monk are guarded. Pagodas, along with statues of Buddha, bells and Buddhist paintings, are

7. Haeinsa Temple in Habcheon, Gyeongsangnam-do Province is one of the "Sambo" (three treasures) Temples of Korea. The Tripitaka Koreana are guarded inside this temple.
8. Songgwangsa Temple in Suncheon, Jeollanam-do Province, is one of the "Sambo" (three treasures) Temples of Korea.
9. The Tripitaka Koreana, designated a World Heritage.

8

9

10

10. Bulguksa Temple's Seokgatap pagoda of Buddha.
National Treasure No.21
11. Mireuksa site 9-storied Stone Pagoda. Korea's first stone Buddha pagoda in Iksan.
National Treasure No.11
12. Bulguksa Temples's Dabotap pagoda.
National Treasure No.20
13. Woljeongsa Temple's Eight-angle Nine-storied Stone Pagoda in Mt. Odaesan, Gangwon-do Province. National Treasure No. 48.
14. Dancheong of colorful patterns. Dancheong refers to the five-colored patterns used in palaces and Buddhist temples to decorate and make the building last longer.

indispensable objects in temples.
According to *Samguksagi*, a book of ancient Korean history Baekje built a 60-meter 9-storied wooden pagoda in Mireuksa Temple in the early 7th century. Inferring from all this, it is believed that quite a few wooden pagodas were built during the 7th century in the Korean Peninsula. An interesting fact is that Baekje built a wooden pagoda and a stone pagoda in the Mireuksa site. It is probably that up until the mid 7th century, wooden pagodas were the main structures followed by stone pagodas, which were partially coexisting.
The style of the wooden pagodas takes after the Mireuksa site 9-storied Stone Pagoda, which is the origin of Korean stone pagodas. This pagoda is very important because it shows the developing process from wooden to stone pagodas. This is also the oldest and largest remaining pagoda in Korea. Because it suffered some damage, its current height is 14 meter high but it is believed to have been around 29 meter high. The Jeongnimsa site 5-storied Stone Pagoda in Buyeo, which was built around the same time also follows the wooden pagoda style. It is an excellent masterpiece from the Baekje architecture with superior elegance and balance.
During the 8th century, the stone pagodas reached their peak. From this time on, the stone pagodas gradually became smaller, from nine-storied, seven-storied and five-storied to four-angled three-storied pagodas and not further than 10 meters tall. The stone pagodas of this period show an outstandingly high artistic level in all facets including design, balance and decorations. The representative stone pagoda of this period worth mentioning are the Gameunsa site 3-storied Stone Pagoda, Bulguksa's Seokgatap and Dabotap.
Many stone pagodas were built during the Goryeo Dynasty. During the Three Kingdoms Era pagodas were built by the government but during the Goryeo Dynasty period, the nobles and wealthy people built a pagoda with their prayers and desires and donated them to temples. Because the building subjects were all different, there was a variety of styles as well. The typical three-storied pagodas was built along with the five, seven, nine or ten-storied pagodas. Although the four-angled pagoda was the standard, octagonal, hexagonal and round pagodas also began to emerge. The most prominent pagodas are Woljeongsa temple 9-storied Stone Pagoda and the Gyeongcheonsa site 10-storied Stone Pagoda.

Dancheong

Dancheong are the patterns and drawings painted with splendid colors on the eaves or doors of traditional wooden buildings. Dancheong crossed to Korea from China when Buddhism was introduced and spread throughout the country, and were widely used in Korean temples and palaces. While Chinese dancheong give off a rather heavy atmosphere and has dark hues, the Korean dancheong is more lively, colorful and graceful. The Japanese dancheong use only the colors red, black and yellow, which makes them less lively than the Korean ones.

The dancheong were used not only for decorative purposes but also for preservation. The patterns on the dancheong use five cardinal colors, which are green, yellow, red, white and black. Flowers and animals were drawn with these colors following a certain order and structure. Korean dancheong can be divided into two main types: the palace dancheong and the temple dancheong. Palace dancheong were made to emit a grandiose and authoritative but polite and refined air while the temple dancheong were drawn to give a mysterious and strong ritual sense.

Jongmyo Shrine

Jongmyo are the royal palace's Confucian shrines that house the ancestral tablets of Joseon kings and queens, similar to the Greek Parthenon. The ideology and order of Confucianism is well expressed architecturally in the structures of Jongmyo.

1. Ceremonial deep bow performed by the royal king to his ancestors.
2. A view of Jongmyo Shrine.

For Koreans rites are essential and sacred ceremonies that pay tribute to their ancestors and are important events for finding one's reason for existence and identity. Since ancient times, Koreans believed that the spirit of their ancestors did not leave this earth but stayed by their descendant's side even after they passed away.

These customs were also carried on in the royal palaces. Particularly, the Joseon Dynasty's royal palace, where the governing ideology of Confucianism considered 'ye', or etiquette a central part in their lives, made ancestral rites a national event. After founding Joseon, building palaces and fortresses, Yi Seonggye built Jongmyo in present day Hunjeong-dong, Jongno-gu, Seoul.

Jongmyo are the royal palace's Confucian shrines that house the ancestral tablets of Joseon kings and queens, similar to the Greek Parthenon. The ideology and order of Confucianism is well expressed architecturally in the structures of Jongmyo. Graceful but highly restrained and using the technique of omitting is the main theme of the Jongmyo architecture. This is why elaborate decoration is omitted and only necessary ornamentation is found. The colors and patterns of the dancheong are also very restrained. Brevity and simplicity make Jongmyo's image even more grave, solemn and sacred. Jongmyo is made up of the main building called Jeongjeon (Main hall) and several annexed shrines including the secondary shrine called Yeongnyeongjeon (Hall of Eternal Peace). The entire Jongmyo is 18.7 hectare wide.

The reason Jongmyo is a precious cultural heritage to Koreans is because of Jongmyo-Jerye, the most elegant and refined ritual ceremony performed within this beautifully artistic area. Jongmyojerye was a solemn national ancestral rite performed by the Joseon royal family according to Confucian standards and was a rite personally supported by the king. Because filial piety, the basic concept of Confucianism was observed at a nation-level, the rites were performed very strictly and solemnly.

While the ancestral rites were being performed, music, song and dance composed this austere atmosphere. The royal ancestral ritual music is called Jongmyojeryeak. The solemn music notes of Jongmyojeryeak rang through the skies and the earth, and called the ancestor spirits. The musical instruments used here are percussion instruments, wind instruments and instruments that composed the tempo of the music. Songs filled with praise to

3

4

the great king's achievements (founding and developing the nation) as well as dance performances were accompanied by various instruments that played a melody. The dance choreography was also very simple and solemn.

This Jongmyo ritual is still performed once a year in Jongmyo, and fills Koreans with a lot of pride. Every May, the Yi (Lee) family from Jeonju or the descendants of the royal family, gather in Jongmyo and perform the ancestral ritual to revive this 600 year-old tradition.

As it is the standard of Confucian shrines, Jongmyo is probably the oldest comprehensive rite cultural heritage in the world harmonizing space for ritual ceremonies, ritual formalities and process, ritual food, utensils used for rituals, ritual instruments and equipment as well as ritual music and dance. Recognizing the enormous value of Jongmyo architecture and the Confucian traditions expressed in them with its traditional rituals that remain intact until today, UNESCO has made it on addition to the World Heritage list.

3. A scene of ancestral rites being performed in Jongmyo where the ancestral tablets of the former Kings and Queens of the Joseon Dynasty are guarded.
4. Dance performance praising the public works of former Korean kings.
5. Gamsil(niche), keeping an ancestral tablet of king and queen.
6. Musicians performing Jongmyo-jeryeak.
7. Sajikdan, guardian deities that prayed for abundance of harvest and performed ancestral rites to the gods of fields and crops during the Joseon Dynasty.

Sajikdan Altar

Sajik is the god of land and crops considered very important in the Korean farming culture. Because the Joseon Dynasty revered Confucian traditions, it made Jongmyo and Sajik the foundation of the national and always did everything to protect these customs.

When King Taejo (Yi Seonggye) found the Joseon Dynasty and built Gyeongbokgung Palace, he put Jongmyo in the east and Sajikdan in the west (present day Sajik Park). Also he held ancestral rites in Jongmyo and let the forefathers know about the foundation of a new nation and held ancestral rites in Sajikdan to wish for abundance.

Since long ago, the Korean kings performed national ancestral rituals to wish for the nation and people's well-being and abundant harvest. This performance was called Sajikdaeje, and the place for its performance was called Sajikdan. Rites were usually performed twice a year in Sajikdan usually, on February and August. When national disasters such as wars or droughts occurred, rituals were also performed here.

Hangeul, the Korean alphabet

Hangeul is the name of the alphabet Koreans use every day. It is a scientific alphabet that resembles our speech organs. It is also the most important cultural heritage of Korean history. This alphabet was created in 1443 by King Sejong, the fourth king of the Joseon Dynasty (1392-1910).

consonant	ㄱ	ㄴ	ㄷ	ㄹ	ㅁ	ㅂ	ㅅ	ㅇ	ㅌ	ㅋ	ㅍ	ㅈ	ㅊ	ㅎ
	g, k	n	d, t	r, l	m	b, p	s	ng	t	k	p	j	ch	h
vowel	ㅏ	ㅑ	ㅓ	ㅕ	ㅗ	ㅛ	ㅜ	ㅠ	ㅡ	ㅣ				
	a	ya	eo	yeo	o	yo	u	yu	eu	i				

2

Hangeul is the name of the alphabet Koreans use every day. It is a scientific alphabet that resembles our speech organs. It is also the most important cultural heritage of the Korean history. This alphabet was created in 1443 by King Sejong, the fourth king of the Joseon Dynasty (1392-1910), and published in 1446 with the name Hunminjeongeum which means 'the proper phonetic system to educate the people'. The first alphabet had 28 letters but only 24 of them are used today.

Hangeul is a scientific alphabet that resembles our speech organs. The shape of the consonants is based on the shape the speech organ makes when that sound is articulated. The vowels resemble the roundness of the sky(·), the flatness of the earth(ㅡ) and a person standing(ㅣ). Hangeul is composed of 10 vowels and 14 consonants and it is a language that was very uniquely and originally made.

The purpose of Hangeul, its creator and the time it was created are all certain. There are around 6,000 languages in the world and only 100 of these have a written alphabet. However no one knows the purpose for its creation, its creator or time of creation. Only Hangeul is certain of all three.

Each and every letter of Hangeul possesses only one sound. If you combine one consonant with one vowel it becomes one syllable. Because the principles of Hangeul are so simple, most Korean children master Hangeul and learn to read before they enter elementary school and this is why Korea is the country with the lowest illiteracy rate in the world.

Hangeul also has abundant expressiveness, probably more than any other language in the world. Therefore, there is an incredibly wide range of words you can choose from to express yourself, for instance, the mood or emotion of a person or the shape of an object. The Korean language has several words and phrases that cannot be translated to foreign languages. This is not because Korean is an inefficient language but because there are no appropriate words in foreign languages capable of conveying the meaning of that specific word.

In addition, Hangeul is an alphabet that can

1. Hunminjeongeum (The proper phonetic system to educate the people) is a book containing the background to the creation of the Korean language and its method of use. National Treasure No. 70.
2. The Korean alphabet. The upper line shows the consonants and the lower line shows the vowels.

3. A recent reenactment of scholars creating Hangeul (Korean language) in Jiphyeonjeon (academic research institute).

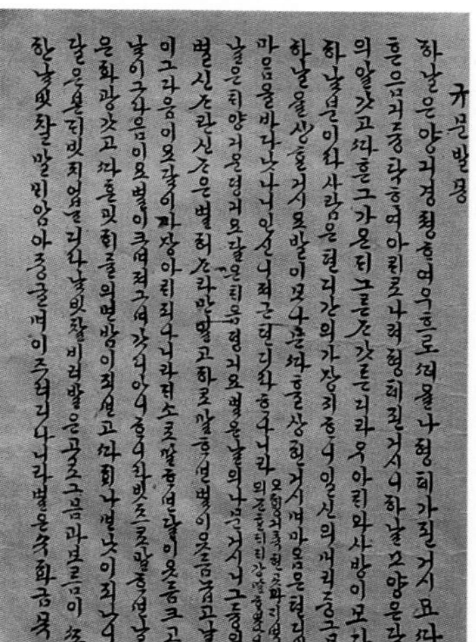

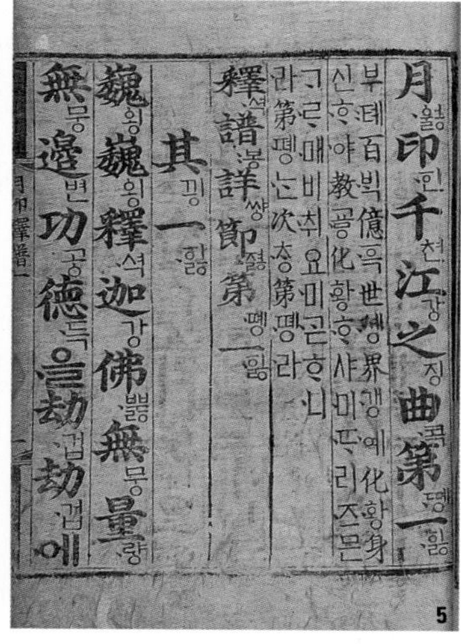

月印千江之曲第一

釋譜詳節第一

其一

巍巍釋迦佛無量

無邊功德을劫劫에

almost perfectly express the sounds of the English language. Hangeul is 20 times more capable of articulating sounds than Chinese or Japanese. For example, there are no accurate letters that can express the brand name "Coca Cola" in Chinese or Japanese. However, Korean can express the word "Coca Cola" perfectly, just as it sounds in English. This is why, as if to show proof of this, Hunminjeongeum (National Treasure No. 70.), a book explaining the principle of Hangeul and the usage of Hangeul, argues that with this alphabet anyone can write any sound including the sound of the wind, the cry of the cranes and rooster, and even the bark of a dog. We can say that Hangeul is the alphabet that can express the most sounds in the world.

In 1994, an article on the 6th Edition of the famous Discovery Magazine introduced Hangeul as the alphabet that is easiest to write with in the world. Famous American writer Pearl Buck called Hangeul "the most simple yet excellent alphabet in the world" and praised King Sejong by calling him the "Korean Leonardo Da Vinci". Hangeul means "the greatest alphabet" in Korean.

4. Hangeul (Korean language) written with a brush and ink.
5. Weolincheongangjigok, a book about the life of Buddha and the first book to be written in the Korean language. Treasure No. 398.
6. Image of King Sejong(1397-1450), creator of the Korean language.

King Sejong

King Sejong(1397-1450) is the fourth king of the Joseon Dynasty and creator of the Korean alphabet. He was the greatest ruler in Korean history. Being the most educated king of the kings in Korean history, he made the utmost effort to use knowledge and education for the people.

Many of the scientific heritages from the Joseon Dynasty displayed in Korean museums were made during King Sejong's reign. King Sejong left countless contributions in many fields including academics, politics, economics, diplomacy, military area, music and printing. In tribute to him, Koreans use his name to christen streets, buildings, research centers, hotels and university. The most famous ones are Sejongno(Sejong Avenue), the Sejong Center, the Sejong Research Institute and the King Sejong Station in Antarctica. In this manner, Koreans engrave his name everywhere and live remembering that they were fortunate to have a great king like him.

The royal tomb of King Sejong can be seen in Yeoju, Gyeonggi-do Province and is called Yeongneung. At the entrance of the tomb, there is an exhibition of his legacy.

Hwaseong Fortress

Hwaseong Fortress is a summary of oriental and western fortification technology. This is why it carries a great significance in architectural history and is considered to be the epitome of 18th century fortress building technology. This fortress was designated a World Heritage by UNESCO in 1997.

분양

Hwaseong is a huge fortress located in Suwon, Gyeonggi-do Province. It is 5.74 kilometer long and covers an area of 130 hectare . King Jeongjo, the 22nd king of the Joseon Dynasty, built this fortification when he moved the grave of his father, Prince Sado, from the outskirts of Seoul to Suwon. By the order of King Jeongjo, a civil servant called Jeong Yakyong built the Hwaseong Fortress according to the instructions in "Principles of Fortress Construction", a book containing oriental and western architecture technology. Construction was started on January 1794 and completed in September 1796.

Hwaseong Fortress is a summary of oriental and western fortification technology. This is why it carries a great significance in architectural history and is considered to be the epitome of 18th century fortress building technology. The outside of the fortress is made of stone piles and the inside was filled with mud soil. The harmony between the stones and soil is uncommon. Also the structures inside the fortress all have different shapes and designs. New architecture technologies from the school of "pragmatic philosophy" or "Silhak," which aimed in finding truth in the real life of the people, was reflected on the construction of this fortress. Also new-developed construction equipment called "goejunggi" or crane was used for the first time. As a result, what originally was thought to take ten years only took 34 months to build.

Korean fortresses are made up mostly of mountain fortress walls, used as refuge during war, and town fortresses(eupseong), which surround the village where people live. Hwaseong was a multi-purpose new city that was the living space for the common people but that also included watchtowers, shooting holes, military commanding posts and communication facilities. Another characteristic of Hwaseong is that roads, the infrastructure of any city, were built centered on the fortress, and along these roads many stores and markets were formed. This fortress is Joseon Dynasty's fine masterpiece that combined artificiality and nature, technology and art, foreign culture with traditional culture and normal and emergency time functions all together.

The Hwaseong Fortress carries a special meaning for Koreans because the breath of an individual that wants us to understand why this fortress was built can be felt everywhere. The name of that individual is King Jeongjo, a sovereign who ruled over the most fierce yet lonely reign of the Joseon Dynasty. It is impossible to understand King Jongjeo's life if you separate Hwaseong Fortress from it.

His great mind and spirit, his personal solitude and strict nature as a king gave birth to the beautiful Hwaseong Fortress. Today, King Jeongjo is the second most praised king of the Joseon Dynasty after King Sejong. King Jeongjo ruled Joseon for only 24 years. However, in that brief time he

1. Night view of Hwaseong Fortress, Suwon. Wonderful sight where traditional and modern buildings can be seen together.
2. A view of Paldalmun Gate which appeared in Hwaseong Seongyeok Uigwe, the Archives of the Construction of Hwaseong Fortress.
3. A complete view of Hwaseong Fortress which appeared in Hwaseong Seongyeok Uigwe, the Archives of the Construction of Hwaseong Fortress.
4. Picture recreating a scene of a military training event.

4

worked endlessly to moder-nize Joseon, to remove tensions between political powers and establish political stability in the kingdom. He was a strong yet wise king. This powerful strength came from the dishonorable death faced by his father, Prince Sado, who died without ascending the throne. At times misfortune can give people strength.

During the late 18th century, the opposition of political factions was at their worst. King Yeongjo, King Jeongjo's grandfather, had been troubled with these political quarrels prior to becoming king. When he assumed the throne, he tried to stabilize the nation by appointing talented men from every party. But Prince Sado, who became entangled in the political fights but was expected to become a great king, was put in a rice chest and left to die of hunger by his own father. King Jeongjo, then 10 years old, had to watch his father die in agony under

5. Paldalmun, one of the gates to Hwaseong Fortress in Suwon.

5

6. Picture recreating a scene of King Jeongjo's march to Hwaseong Fortress.
7. Banghwasuryujeong Hall and its beautiful pond.

the hot sun. After a 52-year rule, King Yeongjo passed the throne onto his grandson, King Jeongjo. However Prince Sado's misfortunate death was an unbreakable obstacle to King Jeongjo as much as it was for King Yeongjo. Not only was King Jeongjo constantly challenged by his subjects about the legitimacy of his reign, but he also suffered because of his parent's misfortunate life. This is why during his entire reign he made filial piety and memorial events an important part of political ethics and accomplished his aims (aspirations).

What he needed the most as a king were loyal subjects, and military and financial power. He also knew that if he wanted to get this, he would need a new political ground other than Seoul where there were no former political powers. He moved his father's grave from Mt. Baebongsan in Jeonnong-dong, Dongdaemun-gu in Seoul to Suwon and started building a new city that would be his political grounds. The person that desired to build the Hwaseong Fortress was King Jeongjo, but the central figure that designed and took part in the construction was the mid-Joseon Silhak scholar Jeong Yakyong. Silhak is a philosophy that received influences from Western thinkers and natural sciences and whose aim is to search for truths that are useful in real life. This school of thought was lead mostly by Sadaebu (or gentlemen scholars) with reformist tendencies. Jeong Yakyong built the geojunggi, which works much like the present day crane. Thanks to this new construction equipment, he was able to perfectly build the new city in a short period of time. The Suwon Hwaseong Fortress is a wonderful fruit of the Silhak philosophy.

The Hwaseong Fortress clearly demonstrates the cultural capacity and science and technology in the late 18th century of the Joseon Dynasty. Architects around the world call Hwaseong Fortress the gem of architecture because it has a scientific and rational structure that satisfies both military defense functions and commercial functions for the common people.

This fortress was designated a World Heritage by UNESCO in 1997 for its high scientific, architectural, artistic, military and humanist value. The document that played a big role designating this fortress a World Heritage were the Archives of the Construction of Hwaseong Fortress(Hwaseong Seongyeok Uigwe). These documents record every detail of the project, from blueprints, work progress, personal information of the workforce budget and wages to construction equipment, required materials and construction journals. What was difficult to express with words was expressed with drawings. It also meticulously records the characteristics of each facility, construction method and fortress building techniques. These archives are a "new" Hwaseong Fortress built on paper. No other city in the world, for instance Russia's St. Petersburg or US's Washington D.C., that was built around the time Hwaseong Fortress was built, that possesses a perfectly detailed, three dimensional construction blueprint of their own city.

Every fall, there is a festival with a reenactment of King Jeongjo's Hwaseong Fortress parade.

The Hahoe Folk Village

There are several folk villages nationwide in Korea. The folk villages are unique places where you can see the people maintaining their old way of life. As a result, these villages are more than the reproduction of a simple traditional village. They are the true original images and identity of the Korean people.

Folk villages are another type of nature with mountains, rivers, wide fields and people. Although today Koreans live in modern homes, the warm and tender folk villages live and breathe inside all of them. There are several folk villages nationwide in Korea. The folk villages are unique places where you can see the people maintain their old way of life. As a result, these villages are more than the reproduction of a simple traditional village. They are the true original images and identity of the Korean people. One of the most representative places is the Hahoe Folk Village in Andong, Gyeongsangbuk-do Province.

Andong is a city where Confucian philosophy and traditional culture still breathes, which is why it is called the capital city of the culture of the Korean spirit. In May 1999, when Queen Elizabeth II visited Korea, she stopped by the small city of Andong and this became the talk of the town at that time. What she probably wanted to see was not Andong itself, but the most Korean images, or the typical Korean traditions and lifestyle culture.

The Hahoe Folk Village is a typical village that shows the social conditions during the Joseon Period. The village is nestled along the Nakdonggang River with its tributaries flowing and surrounding the village, which according to oriental geomancy is called the "floating lotus flower" type of topography. This is because the village appears to be a lotus flower floating on the water.

Huge tile-roofed homes and small straw-thatched homes coexist in this village. The tile roofs are for the yangban or ruling class and the thatched homes for the commoners. Nearby the village were large, wide farmlands. The owner of these lands were the Pungsan Yu clan, who founded a family neighborhood in the Hahoe Village. The common people worked and earned their living from this farmland. More than a hundred traditional homes can be found in Hahoe Village and people still dwell in them. Among these, ten homes including Yangjingdang, Chunghyodang and Hadonggotaek were named Important Folklore Material by the Korean Government. The Hahoe Folk Village is registered in the temporary list of UNESCO's World Heritages.

The beautiful and sentimental atmosphere given by the surrounding mountains and meandering rivers gave a lot of inspiration to the people living in the village. This sensibility produced an immortal masterpiece called Hahoetalnori or Hahoe Mask Dance which

1. People wearing traditional rite uniforms wait to perform ancestral rites.
2. View of Hahoe Folk Village with thatched-roof homes and roof-tile homes

3

國泰民安
歲和年豐
4

possesses abundant artistic value. The Hahoe Mask Dance was a drama lampooning the contradictory hierarchical society. Since 800 years ago, the people put on masks and held a festival that lampooned or criticized the yangban's hypocrisy and contradictions. The yangban could understand the people's lives and daily hardships through these masked performances. As a result, they produced the Hahoe community. This mask dance is still held every fall. The masks used in these performances are called Hahoe Masks. The Hahoe Mask is the only mask that has been designated a Korean National Treasure. This mask humorously and uniquely expresses the laughing and crying expressions of Koreans and therefore has been recognized as world-level mask. If you want to get more detailed information on the yangban and commoners' way of life during the Joseon period, visit the Andong Folk Museum. This museum recreated the important ceremonies (marriage, funeral, etc), folk games, and diverse traditional homes which all show the characteristics of Confucian culture.

3. A scene of the Hahoe Mask Drama.
4. View of Hahoe Folk Village's traditional homes.
5. A performer wearing a 'bunei tal' (gisaeng's mask).
6. Yangban (gentleman)'s mask, a type of hahoe mask.
7. 'Gaksi tal' (woman's mask), a type of hahoe mask.
8. Naganeupseong Folk Village in Suncheon, Jeollanam-do Province.

Other Folk Villages

The Korean Folk Village The Korean Folk Village is in Yongin, Gyeonggi-do Province, the outskirts of Seoul. This folk village soundly and accurately recreated the life of ancient Korea in a space of 72 hectare. In addition, you can see many ancient customs and performances such as nongak(farm music), jultagi(rope walking) and Korean traditional weddings. If you visit the traditional markets you can try Korean traditional foods.

Naganeupseong Folk Village. The Nagan village in Nagan-myeon, Suncheon, Jeollanam-do Province has the mood and atmosphere of the Korean old rural villages preserved intact. Naganeupseong is a fortress built in the vast fields of the people's land. Within the fortress are government buildings and around a hundred straw-thatched homes. Many of the homes were designated Important Folklore Material by the government. Besides this, you can visit the Oeam-ri Folk Village in Asan, Chungcheongnam-do Province, the Seongeup Folk Village in Jejudo Island. The Yangdong Folk Village in Gyeongju, Gyeongsangbuk-do Province, the latter is on the temporary list of World Heritage.

Art & Tradition

Hanbok

ⓒ Lee Younghee

1

The hanbok is a beautiful costume that contains the spirit of Koreans. The history of the hanbok goes back to the Three Kingdoms Period(18 BC - 660 AD). The hanbok is an outfit that harmoniously combines straight and curved lines. The edge of the *chima* or skirt moves gracefully with a soft breeze, and because of the beautiful silhouette it shapes, particularly on the women's hanbok, the hanbok has been dubbed "the costume of the wind".

The *hanbok* is the Korean traditional attire. It used to be worn customarily by Koreans every day but nowadays it is usually worn on special family occasions or big holidays. The history of the hanbok goes back to the Three Kingdoms Period(18 BC–660 AD). You can see the first hanbok inside the Goguryeo mural paintings in Manchuria and North Korea. If you take a look at the costumes worn by the people depicted in the mural paintings, the upper garments or *jeogori*(coat) fall below the waist, and the width of the *baji*(pants) is quite narrow. The *chima*(skirt) is long, and the Korean *durumagi*(overcoat) is only knee-high. These costumes are also quite colorful. The hanbok sought convenience and aesthetic beauty at the same time.

The components of the hanbok(jeogori, chima, baji and durumagi) and the pursuit of a harmonious combination of straight and curved lines remains almost unchanged since the Three Kingdoms Period. However the length, width, patterns and colors of the costume has changed noticeably.

There are many types of hanbok. First there is the ceremonial hanbok and the regular hanbok. Although this is not the case today in the old times, the royals and nobles wore different types of hanbok than the commoners. The hanboks were also classified into women, men and children hanbok.

The hanbok is an outfit that harmoniously combines straight and curved lines. The edge of the chima moves gracefully with a soft breeze, and because of the beautiful silhouette it shapes, particularly on the women's hanbok, it has been dubbed "the costume of the wind".

The beauty produced by the lines and surfaces of the hanbok are very special. Added to the wonderful colors blends, patterns and accessories, the hanbok generates a graceful and splendid atmosphere. Generally the hanbok is arranged in two colors, which follows the principles of the cosmic forces of yin and yang.

There are a variety of fabrics used to make hanbok. Stiff and sturdy material such as linen or hemp fiber are used for summer hanbok. Softer, more elegant thin silks are used for spring and fall hanbok and refined and warmer material such as Western satin and plain woven silk are used for winter hanbok.

1. Hanbok worn by a Joseon Dynasty(1392-1910) queen on her wedding day.
2. Ceremorial Hanbok worn on a Korean typical wedding day currently.

ⓒ Lee Younghee

2

3

4

When you wear a hanbok, your body movements and gestures automatically become more careful and reserved. This is because the hanbok is more than just a simple dress but a garment imbued with the spirit and etiquette of the oriental culture. Although the design, color and patterns of the hanbok changed according to the social status and gender, the main significance of each of these clothes has been the same.

The kings and princes of the Joseon Period (1392–1910) wore the royal hanbok while the palace officials wore hanbok of different colors and patterns according to their rank. Similar to the men's hanbok, the women's hanbok differed according to their rank and position. A significant difference is that, unlike the men, they wore several undergarments, usually four or five. Common men and women usually wore white clothes during regular times. However ceremonial dress was worn during ancestral rites or wedding ceremonies. In addition, when people went out they put on the *durumagi* overcoat.

The hanbok is a beautiful costume that contains the spirit of Koreans. According to the time period, the length of the *jeogori* as well as the width of the sleeves and the *chima* have changed slightly, which produced today's hanbok. Today, Koreans generally wear the hanbok during special events since most people prefer to wear the more comfortable western style clothing instead. However hanbok designers have developed a new modified version of hanbok that adds practicality to the advantages of the hanbok. This new hanbok is called *saenghwal hanbok*(literally "lifestyle hanbok"). Saenghwal hanbok, also called *gaeryang hanbok*, is the fruit of the hard work of designers trying to find a way to make hanbok more practical and convenient to wear. Nowadays you can see many people on the streets wearing these new "lifestyle hanbok" particularly writers, traditional artists and scholars.

In addition, fashion designers are working very hard to make hanbok an international costume. They are applying the lines and patterns of the traditional hanbok into the modern day fashion and creating a new fashion from it.

3. Engraved seal prints recreating the traditional costume shown in the Goguryeo Kingdom (37 BC – 668 AC) tomb wall paintings, Jung Byung-rye, 2004.
4. Fomal attire of civil officials, Joseon Dynasty, Baek Jee-hye, 2004.
5. Korean modern women's hanbok today.
6. *Nubi jeogori*, coat and *beoseon*, Korean socks for winter use.
7. Korean women wearing casual clothes today.

5

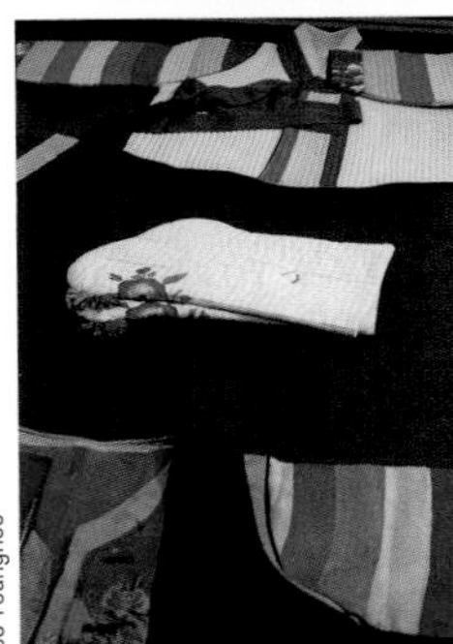

6

7

Kimchi

Kimchi is the most popular Korean food. Kimchi signifies 'vegetables fermented in salt' in Korean. There are various main ingredients of kimchi including Chinese cabbages, turnips, pumpkins, eggplants, sesame leaves, Korean lettuce and stone leeks. To Koreans, kimchi is something more than just food.

2

Korean food is divided mainly into main dishes and side dishes. Rice is the staple main dish and is accompanied by several *banchan* or side dishes. *Kimchi*, *bulgogi*, soups and stews made with all types of vegetables and meats, roasted fish and steamed vegetables are some examples of side dishes.

Kimchi is the most popular Korean food. Kimchi signifies "vegetables fermented in salt". There are various main ingredients of kimchi including Chinese cabbages, turnips, pumpkins, eggplants, sesame leaves, Korean lettuce and stone leeks. In other words, most vegetables are ingredients of kimchi. Add salt, garlic, Cayenne pepper powder, ginger, pickled fish or shrimp, pear juice and chestnuts to the vegetables and you will have completed a kimchi dish.

In the past, kimchi was simply vegetables stored in salt. For a long time, only a few spices were added to this basic kimchi. In the 1600s Cayenne peppers and pickled fish were introduced as main ingredients to kimchi. And in the modern age, pears, chestnuts and pine nuts have been added to this dish.

Kimchi is such an important food to Koreans that there is even a popular song about kimchi. The first lyrics to the song are, "If we didn't have kimchi, how tasteless rice would be. Even if they tempt me with delicacies and gourmet meals, without kimchi, there will always be something missing." Kimchi is the staple food that Koreans eat throughout their entire lives. It also represents the Korean sentiment, culture and is a definition of their identity. To Koreans, kimchi is something more than just food.

Kimchi also surpasses the historical value of other foods. In the section called *Weizhi dongyizhuan* of the book of *Sanguozhi*(history book of ancient China) that explains the food of Goguryeo, it mentions that "the people of Goguryeo use salt when eating vegetables, and they have excellent fermentations skills". According to this record, the history of kimchi is considered to be at least 1,500 to 2,000 years old.

There are numerous types of kimchi. Kimchi is classified generally according to the vegetables it uses as its main ingredient. For example, if *baechu* (Chinese cabbage) is used as the main ingredient it is called *baechu kimchi* (Chinese cabbage kimchi), if the main ingredient is *mu*

1. Kimchi is the most prominent Korean fermented dish. The upper dish is of baechu kimchi or Chinese cabbage kimchi and the lower dish is of mu kimchi or raddish kimchi.
2. Dongchimi, a type of raddish kimchi, is very popular for its refreshing taste.

3. *Baechu* or Chinese cabbage and pa or leek, the main ingredients of kimchi.
4. *Insam*, which contains the meaning of panacea in Korea.
5. Gochu or red cayenne peppers, a main ingredient of kimchi.
6. A farmer woman is smiling while harvesting raddish, one of the main ingredients of kimchi.
7. Making baechu kimchi or Chinese cabbage kimchi.
8. *Yakju*, Korean traditional wine.

(raddish) it is called *mu kimchi* (turnip kimchi). However, even if the same vegetable is used as the main ingredient, the kimchi can be called a different way according to the method of preparation. Following is a more detailed explanation of kimchi.

Baechu kimchi(Chinese cabbage kimchi): After cutting the cabbage into two or four parts, the cabbage is soaked and stored in salted water and fermented with various garnishes.

Chonggak kimchi: After soaking altarimu (ponytail raddish) in salt, spices are added and then left to ferment.

Kkakdugi: After the then turnip is cut into small bite-size cubes, it is soaked in salt water with spices and left to ferment.

Apart from this, there are various types of baechu(cabbage) or mu(turnip or raddish) kimchi. There are kimchi made of other types of vegetables as well. Sesame leaf kimchi, parsley kimchi, Korean lettuce kimchi, stone-leek kimchi, leek kimchi, cucumber kimchi, eggplant kimchi, and cabbage kimchi are the most notable ones.

Kimchi is tastiest when it is stored for a while at around 5°C. In the past, Koreans dug holes in the ground and kept the kimchi in large jars under-

Korean Insam

The root of *Insam*, which curiously resembles the shape of the human body, is a plant that is used for medical purposes. In English, it is called *Korean Insam* while its scientific name is *Panax Ginseng C. A. Meyer*. Here *panax* stands for a panacea or a cure for all diseases. In short, Korean *Insam* is considered to be the best in the world.

Insam was first introduced to the western world through a Dutch merchant in 1610. It was introduced to England through the East Indies Company. The Korean *Insam* was a precious and valuable local product famous enough to be offered to Louis the XIV. According to his biography, Jean Jacques Russeau, the famous author of *Emille*, is said to have been a *Insam* lover during his lifetime. According to recent studies, *Insam* also relieves fatigue, stress, arteosclerosis, it lowers your blood pressure and your sugar level, has an anti-ageing effect, improves virility or stamina and even treats alcohol addictions. It is also used to treat all types of skin problems such as acne, skin discoloration, freckles, and athlete's foot.

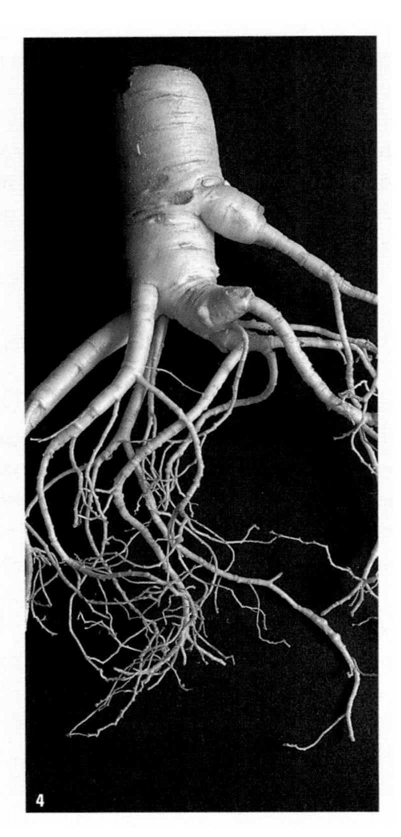

ground. This was a perfect way to store kimchi, because the temperature underground always remains the same becoming the perfect environment for microorganisms to breed fast, enhancing the taste of kimchi. In recent years, a kimchi refrigerator has been developed and sold extensively. Today, many Korean homes use kimchi refrigerators.

Kimchi is a main source of nutrients such as proteins, vitamins and minerals. It enhances your appetite and is a great alkaline that aids digestion. It keeps your intestines healthy and has an anti-bacterial effect. The ingredients used to spice kimchi such as garlic, peppers and ginger have been proven effective in preventing cancer and heart disease. Not long ago, Korea received the spotlight and caused a stir in the media because it was the only country in Asia that did not have any patients who tested positive with SARS when SARS was spreading everywhere else in the world. Medical scientists believe that kimchi contains a virus-resistant effect. As the wonderful effects of kimchi are being scientifically proven, it is finding its place as a popular dish around the world.

Korean Liquors

The most representative traditional drinks in Korea are *takju, yakju* and *soju.* Among these, takju has the oldest history. Takju is made by putting malted wheat and water in steamed rice and then leaving it to ferment. The alcoholic content is around 6-7 percent. In Korea, takju means that the liquor is not clear but turbid. Takju is commonly known as *makgeolli* in Korea. Yakju is clear liquor made by removing the remnants of the takju after it is almost completely fermented. Although soju was more popular than takju, it became a popular drink again after the 1990s. The most representative takju alcoholic beverages are bekseju and sansachun. Soju is the product of the effort to overcome the disadvantage of fermented liquors, not being able to be stored for prolonged periods. The answer was distilling these fermented liquors. There are two types of Korean soju: diluted soju and distilled soju. Diluted soju is more inexpensive than distilled soju and is a popular drink that most Koreans enjoy drinking. The alcohol content is 22–24 percent. The distilled soju has a stronger scent than the diluted soju and a far more refined taste. The most representative ones are Andong soju from the city of Andong, Munbaeju from Seoul, and Igangju from Jeonju, Joellabuk-do Province. The alcohol content is 40-45 percent.

© Baesangmyun breuery

Taekwondo

Taekwondo is the Korean traditional martial arts. Today Taekwondo has found its place in the world of martial arts related to body and mind training. Taekwondo was first recognized as an official sport event during the 1988 Summer Olympics. Now there are around 5 million people learning taekwondo around the world.

Taekwondo is a combination of three words, *tae*, *kwon* and *do*. *Tae* represent the foot techniques, *kwon* represent hand techniques and *do* signifies intuition or mind. If we put these together, tae and kwon signify physical exercises and do signifies the mental training. *Taekwon* is the dynamic world and *do* is the static world, *taekwon* is the metaphysical world while *do* is the physical world. According to the theory of *eum* and *yang*, *taekwon* is negative or minus and *do* is positive or plus. Therefore, putting everything in order, taekwondo is a sport and martial art where the body and mind, dynamic and static worlds, metaphysical and physical words, positive and negative worlds must meet to be completed. The reason why taekwondo is called a sport where the body and mind are disciplined lies here.

Taekwondo is often called one of the performing art that contains the Korean spirit. The beauty of this art can be divided into two parts, the dynamic beauty and the static beauty. The static beauty is the mental aspect of taekwondo discipline, in other words, "the static state of being still and quiet". This can be called contemplation or meditation. The dynamic beauty is emitted through movements. Body movements such as kicking, hitting and thrusting are not just simple fighting movement. These are ways of expressing your mind, spirit and ideas with your body. In this aspect, taekwondo has similar principles to those of dance movements.

The origins of taekwondo go as far back as the prehistoric age. Unfortunately, there are not records or historical remains on taekwondo proving this. However, the true image of taekwondo can be seen properly on the cultural remains of the Three Kingdoms Period(18 BC–660 AD). Around the 5th century, Goguryeo people drew people doing taekwondo in the wall paintings of the ancient mounds. Taekwondo went under the different name of *taekkyoen* back then. Among the figures in the Seokguram grotto in Gyeongju, you can see the faces of Silla(57 BC–927 AD) ancient martial arts masters. In the Bunhwangsa stone pagoda in Gyeongju similar figures are also visible. There are innumerable records related to taekwondo of the Goryeo(918

1. A tomb mural of the Goguryeo Kingdom(37 BC-668 AD) depicting a martial arts competition. This picture shows the origins of taekwondo.
2. Olympic gold medal winner Mun Daeseong during the 2004 Athens Olympic Games (right).

3
© Lee Kabchul

4
© AP photo

© Yonhap News

© AP photo

–1392) or Joseon Period(1392 - 1910).

Taekwondo also has a technique structure called *pumsae*(movement sequences). *Pumsae* sums up the entire basic attack or defense movements according to training levels. These movements include *seogi*(ready stance), *makgi* (defense or blocking), *jjireugi* (thrusting) and *chagi*(kicking).

There are a total of 17 pumsae or levels in taekwondo. In other words, taekwondo is divided into 17 levels according to how the level of training or ability the student has received. A beginner student would learn the first pumsae, while a master would learn the 17th pumsae. Pumsae is similar to the *dan* system used to categorize students according to their level of training. There are also 17 levels in the dan system. If you reach the 11th level, you are given the qualifications to be a taekwondo instructor. It takes endless hours of training and meditation for a novice to reach this level of mastery; some say it takes more than 10 years. The basic taekwondo uniform consists of white pants, white coat and a black belt tied around the waist. The pants, coat and belt compose the taekwondo uniform set. There are five belt colors of taekwondo, which are white, yellow, blue, red and black. Novices wear white, intermediate level students wear yellow, red or blue and masters who have reached 9th level or above wear black belts.

Taekwondo is basically divided into *pumsae* (form), *gyeorugi*(competition) and *gyeokpa* (breaking). As mentioned above, pumsae are the movement sequences that allow you to connect attack and defense movents with gyeorugi. Gyeorugi is the struggle or competition done between two competitors using the basic skills acquired from the pumsae structure. Gyeokpa is the technique that uses hands and feet to break wooden blocks, tiles and bricks.

Taekwondo considers *ye*(etiquette), *ki*(energy or spirit) and meditation more important than strength. Particularly, *yejeol*(or the rules of etiquette) are considered the most important aspect of taekwondo. Before and after a competition, competitors bow respectfully to one another. You could say that taekwondo is a sport that begins and ends with ye(etiquette).

3. Geumgangyeoksasang, or temple guardians, engraved in the Gyeongju Bunhwangsa Stone Pagoda. This picture shows the origins of taekwondo.
4. Olympic gold medal winner Mun Daesong shows his balchagi (kick) during the 2004 Athens Olympic Games.
5. Foreign taekwondo masters demonstrating a defensive position in taekwondo
6. Olympic gold medal winner Jang Jiwon during the 2004 Athens Olympic Games (left).

Paintings

1

Petroglyphs(stone paintings) decorate the forefront of Korean painting history. The Three Kingdoms Period(18 BC–660 AD) produced tomb murals and Buddhist paintings. The most representative paintings of the Goryeo Dynasty(918–1392) are the Buddhist paintings. Joseon Dynasty(1392–1910)) has simple and plain Indian ink paintings of natural landscapes instead of ostentatious color displays.

While the Korean Prehistoric age produced petroglyphs, the Three Kingdoms Period produced tomb murals and Buddhist paintings. Particularly, each and every Goguryeo(37 BC–668 AD) tombs can be considered an ancient museum in itself. These fresco style wall paintings show the living conditions, Buddhist and Taoist ideas of that period. The Goguryeo tomb murals guide us back 1,500 years ago.

The inner structure of the Goguryeo tomb murals is the same as that of common homes of today, and its wall surfaces contain all types of paintings. The themes of most of the paintings during this period are their views of the world and religion as well as the image of the deceased when they were alive. Paintings of men and women servants attending the landlord, going out followed by a long line or parade of people, going hunting accompanied by inferiors all show the material abundance of the landlord (or tomb's owner) during this period. These paintings many represent the desire for the deceased to have continuous abundance in his next life. In these paintings, the lifestyle and living conditions of the Goguryeo society are clearly seen. The costume patterns, the width of the sleeves and legs, the hairstyles and type of hats were drawn differently according to the social status of that person. The Gogur-yeo tomb murals have thick lines, are full of life and imagination. These were named 2004 World Heritages by UNESCO.

According to historical records there were Buddhist paintings and wall paintings in every temple during the Three Kingdoms Period. Tragically, all the structures built during this period have disappeared. Hence we cannot physically see these paintings. Historic books mention that painters from Goguryeo and Baekje crossed to Japan and painted Buddhist paintings and wall paintings there, but these have also disappeared. The existence of these paintings can be confirmed only through historic records in Japan and Korea.

The most prominent paintings of the Goryeo Dynasty(918–1932) are the Buddhist paintings. Goryeo Buddhist paintings are a ideal and Symbolic expression of the Buddhist faith. Paintings of *Amitayeorae*(Amitabha Buddha), *Gwansaeeumbosal*(the Bodhisattva of love and

1. Painter Jeong Seon's(1676-1759) Geumgangjeondo, a painting of Mt. Geumgangsan, National Treasure No. 217, Leeum Museum.
2. Bronze Age petroglyphs (rock paintings), Daegok-ri, Ulsan.
3. Goguryeo tomb wall paintings of a dragon.

前人未發可謂奇

蕙園

4

compassion) and *Jijang Bodhisattva*(the Boddhisattva who rescues suffering souls from Hell) use a lot of red, blue, gold and green, and give a bright and splendid but solemn feeling. The Buddhist paintings of the Goryeo Period made great contributions to the development of Japanese paintings. Presently there are around 70 Buddhist paintings from Goryeo in Japan.

While the Three Kingdoms and Goryeo were Buddhist nations, Joseon(1932 - 1910) was a Confucian nation. Confucianism greatly influenced not only the world of politics, economy and society but also culture and the arts. Scholars and artists of the time thought highly of a righteous and humble life and this way of thinking was reflected entirely in how they viewed aesthetic beauty. Consequently, Joseon has simple and plain Indian ink paintings of natural landscapes instead of ostentatious color displays. Until the mid Joseon period, it adopted painting styles from China, internalized, developed them and created their own painting style. In the late Joseon period, to reflect upon this, exploration of the identity was done continuously.

On the basis of the painting style of this era, Korean mountains and streams and paintings of the daily lives of Koreans through the eyes of Koreans appeared, these were called *Jingyeongsansuhwa* style(landscape paintings) and *pungsokhwa* style(genre paintings). Notable artists of this era are Jeong Seon, the master of Jingyeongsansuhwa paintings as well as Kim Hongdo and Shin Yunbok, masters of pungsokhwa paintings. Inside these painters' drawings you can see beautiful natural landscapes and the daily lives of Korean people.

4. Shin Yunbok's painting of a late Joseon Dynasty gisaeng, female entertainer, The National Museum of Korea.
5. Ssireum or Korean Wrestling, Kim Hongdo(1745-1806) Treasure No. 527, The National Museum of Korea.
6. Kim Hongdo's painting of a dancing boy, Treasure No. 527, The National Museum of Korea.
7. Buddhist paintings painted on the wall of a Buddhist sanctuary, The National Museum of Korea.

Ceramics

Ceramics are the essence of arts and crafts. Along with Chinese ceramics, Korean ceramics are the leaders in the history of ceramics. Korea has been producing ceramics since the 10th century. However Japan started producing ceramics in the 17th century by themselves while Europe started in the 18th century.

Korean ceramics started being produced since the Neolithic Age. The ceramics produced during this period were called comb-pattern earth ceramics. V-shaped surfaces were decorated with parallel lines. At times the direction of the lines crossed each other. The artifacts of this period have more meaning for their practical use than their artistic value. Silla and Gaya's ceramics followed the comb-pattern earth ceramic. There are quite many ceramics that have much decorative and artistic and practical value.

Celadon (greenish porcelain)

If ceramic pottery is the one made in low temperatures, porcelain are glazed with an enamel and made in high temperatures. In other words, procelain is a further developed form of ceramic. Porcelain was first produced in China. Around the 10th century, Goryeo brought the porcelain technology from China and introduced it to its own country during the 12th century and created works that stood out in the world of ceramics. These works usually have a beautiful and radiating greenish color, and diverse and detailed concave or convex patterns. Also the artistic property and the balanced beauty of these ceramics reaches almost perfection. The Chinese people who developed these celadon considered these Goryeo ceramics the best in the world, and they wished to keep one in their homes.
The Goryeo celadon developed even further and evolved into the *sanggamcheongja* porcelain(inlaid celadon). This inlaid celadon is made with a technique developed solely by Goryeo ceramists who got the idea from metal crafting techniques such as the damascening that carves or inlays sanggam patterns with silver thread in the celadon. The appearance of the inlaid celadon brought a numerous variety of patterns compared to the Goryeo celadon. They carved countless patterns such as arabesque patterns dangchomun, lotus flower, peonies, chrysanthemums, phoenixes, cranes, clouds, bamboo trees and leaves. This is how they were able to produce ceramics with different atmosphere, impressions, tastes, moods and texturs. Because of their unique qualities, these celadon made with the inlay technique receive special value and recognition in the history of world ceramics.

1. A ceramist using the spinning wheel to make ceramics.
2. Earth pottery of 'Warrior on Horseback' from the Silla kingdom, National Treasure No. 91, The National Museum of Korea.
3. Goryeo(918-1392) celadon using inlay techniques, Treasure No. 558, Leeum Museum.

At the turn of the 14th century, the inlaid celadon slowly deteriorated and *buncheongjagi* (grayish stoneware) took its place. Along with the Goryeo inlaid celadon, buncheong wares are unique products that exist only in Korea. Bunchoeng wares are inlaid celadon painted with an additional coating of whitish soil. This is why buncheong wares usually give off a grayish color. Buncheong wares were at their peak from the late Goryeo period to the early Joseon period, after the 16th century. The colors, shapes and designs of the buncheong wares are for the masses. The patterns were modern and selected freely. Because the shape, patterns and colors of the bunchoeng wares were not showy they did not receive much appeal or recognition from the common people. However they received a lot of attention from world ceramics experts and ceramic lovers.

At a lecture of a US pottery school, the 20th century world famous potter Bernard Beach said, "what the 20th century modern potters had to accomplish, the buncheong wares have already done. We must make it our goal and follow it." Japanese tea ceremony enthusiasts were fascinated and almost religiously worshipped these buncheong wares. There is even a tale of a Japanese feudal lord who once said he would exchange his small castle for one buncheong ware. Around the mid 16th century, these ceramics, famous for their free

4. Incense burner with perforated chrysanthemum leaves patterns, National Treasure No. 95, The National Museum of Korea.
5. A kettle made with lotus flower patterns, National Treasure No, Lee um Museum.

expression and modern sense gave the spotlight to the Joseon *Baekja* (white celadon).

Baekja(white porcelain)

The Baekja(white porcelain) coexisted with the bunchoeng wares during the 15th century and became the leading pottery of Korea in the 16th century. Baekja is a white-color celadon made with extremely fine white soil. There were several types of baekja including the *sunsubaekja*(pure white celadon) with no patterns or drawings on the surfaces, *cheonghwabaekja*(jade white celadon), a celadon with glazed blue patterns, and *cheolhwabaekja*, patterns painted with wires. The baekja shows a static, simple, lonely and aristocratic beauty. The beauty of restraint and the aesthetic beauty of the blank space contained in the baekja is connected to Confucianism, the leading philosophical mentality of that period.
While Goryeo was a Buddhist nation, Joseon was a Confucian nation. Confucianism greatly influenced not only the world of politics, economy and society but also culture and the arts. Scholars and artists of the time thought highly of a righteous and humble life and this way of thinking was reflected entirely in their concept of aesthetics or beauty. Consequently, Joseon has simple and plain Indian ink paintings of natural landscapes instead of ostentatious color displays or the baekja with its modest and static beauty instead of the colorful Goryeo celadon. Also woodcrafts that maximized natural beauty reached its zenith during this period. The leading philosophy of the Joseon period, which was to build a moral nation on Confucian thought, was reflected entirely in the art works.
The Joseon baekja made a critical contribution in opening the ceramic culture in Japan. Japan invaded Korea during the late 16th century, starting the fierce Imjin Waeran Wars which lasted 7 years. During this war, Japan took around 1,000 Korean ceramic craftsmen by force. Up to that point, Japan lacked the skills and techniques to make ceramics. These craftsmen opened the page of the Japanese ceramic history. Even today, Japanese people deify and look up to these potters and craftsmen.

6. Celadon bottle with embossed bamboo shoots patterns, National Treasure No. 169, Leeum Museum.
7. Buncheong ware tea plate.
8. Buncheong ware plate with peony blossom patterns, Treasure No. 1070, Leeum Museum.
9. Baekja, a work of art characterized by its simple beauty.
10. Cheolhwa baekja with bamboo patterns, Treasure No. 166, The National Museum of Korea.

Handicrafts

Clearly seen from its ceramics, Korea is a nation of arts and crafts. Apart from ceramics, the most important crafts are metal crafts, carpentry, embroidery and paper crafts.

Metal Crafts

The Three Kingdoms Period was the zenith for metallic artifacts. Among the three, Baekje was the kingdom that furthest developed metal crafts to a superior level. The representative works are the royal crowns, gold-plated copper shoes and accessories, metal arts and crafts discovered inside King Muryeong's royal tomb in Gongju, metallic artifacts, a large and long dagger with a dragon and a phoenix, symbols of the king's power, carved on it and the Bronze-gilt Incense Burner of Baekje from Neungsan-ri, considered to be the masterpiece of Baekje's metal craft. Every single metal artifact from the Baekje period is elegant and refined. Also their elaborate details and beauty are of the highest quality.

The early Silla metal crafts such as their royal crowns or jewelry ornaments fell slightly behind Baekje in terms of their artistry and completion degree. On the other hand, the metal crafts made during unified Silla period demonstrate a mature beauty reaching almost perfection. This is because Silla received Goguryeo and Baekje's culture and developed it further. Briefly, the characteristics of the metal crafts during the unified Silla period are unity, harmony and Buddhist beauty sense.

Wood Crafts

If the leading craftwork of the Three Kingdom Period was metal crafts, the leading craftwork of the Goryeo and Joseon period was wood-craft. Except for the lacquer work with mother-of-pearl inlays of *najeonchilgi*, the Goryeo and Joseon woodcrafts are hard to explain. Najeonchilgi are wooden furniture inlaid with mother-of-pearl and painted with lacquer. Along with ceramics, najeonchilgi are the most prominent trade products of the Goryeo Period. The woodcraft of the Goryeo period has a strong, noble and aristocratic tendency, which makes them detailed, luxurious and elegant.

Compared to Goryeo, the Joseon period woodcraft is more modest and favored the taste of the commoners. Although the wood artifacts from the royal family and nobles were splendid and showy with wonderful patterns and drawings on them, they are much less splendid than the Goryeo woodcrafts. Wood-crafts that maxi-mized the natural grain of the

1. Embroidery of flowers and birds.
2. Sarira casket of Gameunsa Temple in Gyeongju.
3. Standing gilt-bronze gwaneum-bosal statue of the Unified Silla Kingdom. Treasure No. 927, Leeum Museum.

wood, which gave way to their restrained and natural beauty was the peak of Joseon Dynasty woodcraft. The focus of Joseon woodcrafts was practical furniture such as cabinets, dressers, small tables and regular tables. For their longer preservation and make these furniture more beautiful, the Joseon wood-craftsmen painted lacquer on them.

Embroidery and Korean paper Crafts

Because of the Joseon women's highly skillful artistic abilities fabric crafts such as *bojagi* (cloth wrappers), embroideries and paper crafts such as boxes with *hanji* or Korean traditional paper were developed. The history of Korean embroidery is estimated to be more than 2,000 years old. History books from China and Korea mention that before the Christian era "aristocrats already walked around with silk clothes embroidered with gold and silver threads". Koreans embroidered clothes, screens, furniture, leather shoes and accessories. Generally the embroidery motifs were flowers, birds, fish, leaves, trees and clouds. They were all elegant and colorful.
There is a Korean proverb that says, "Silk might last 500 years but paper lasts 1,000 years". Koreans already started using paper to make crafts 1,500 years ago. These crafts were made by twisting or weaving paper, macerating the paper in water and mixing it with glue or dyeing several *hanji* with different natural colors and attaching them together. Generally Korean paper craft is completed by adhering a colored pattern made of hanji on the craft piece. Jewelry boxes, small trays, plates, furniture and even Buddhist figures have been made with hanji.

4. Lacquer ware inlaid with mother-of-pearl of the Joseon Dynasty.
5. Embroidered thimbles.
6. Paper fan made with hanji, Korean traditional paper.

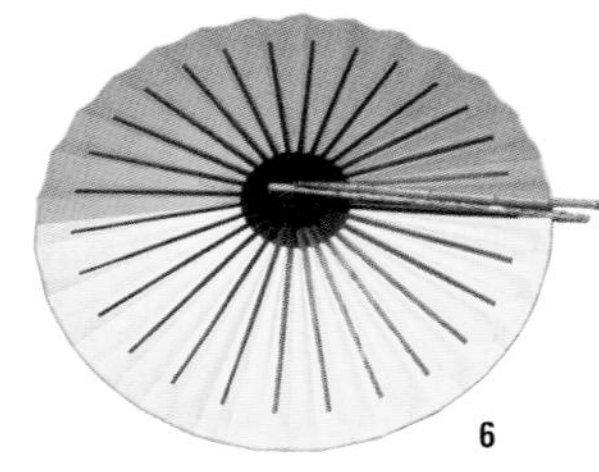

7

7. Embroidery cloud and cranes
8-10. Korean traditional woodcrafts, The National Folk Museum of Korea.

8

9

10

Cities

Seoul

1

Area 605km²
Population 10.28 million
Temperature Average annual temperature is 12.9˚C, January average temperature is 0.3˚C, August average temperature is 24.2˚C

History

Seoul is Korea's capital city. It is an old city with 2,000 years of history. Humans started inhabiting Seoul in the Neolithic period. The pottery artifacts and the habitat of the Neolithic period found in Amsa-dong, Gangdong-gu and Eungbong-dong, Seongdong-gu are proof of this. Seoul appears in history books during the Baekje(18 BC–660 AD) period. Onjo, Baekje's ancestor and king, founded a city at the southern part of the Hangang River. Two earth castles of the Baekje period can be found south of the Hangang River in the Olympic Park and Pungnap-dong. They are *Mongchon-toseong*(Mongchon mud fortress) and *Pungnap-toseong*(Pungnap Mud Fortress). Historians believe Pung-naptoseong was a fortress of the early Baekje Kingdom. Another relic of this period, Baekje's first royal tomb, is found nearby this earthen fortress in Seokchon-dong Songpa-gu.

After Baekje moved its capital to Gongju in Chungcheong-nam-do Province, located in the middle of the peninsula, Seoul became the borderline of Goguryeo(37 BC–668 AD), Silla (57 BC–935 AD) and Baekje. Until the late 600s, all three nations fought fiercely to occupy Seoul. When Silla unified all Three Kingdoms, Seoul became Silla's territory until the early 10th century when it became Goryeo's territory(918-1392). During the Goryeo Dynasty, Seoul was called Namgyeong which means "a capital city in the south that is secondary."

General Yi Seonggye overthrew Goryeo and established a new nation called Joseon. During the Joseon Dynasty (1392–1910), Seoul regained its glory when Joseon decided to make it its capital city and named it Hanyang. Seoul was the first planned city built on *Fengsui Dilishuo* or the geomancy theory. He built fortresses along the four mountains that surround Seoul which are Bugaksan in the north, Naksan in the east, Inwangsan in the west, and Namsan in the south. Beneath Bugaksan he built a palace called Gyeongbokgung Palace. Bugaksan is the mountain behind *Chong Wa Dae* or the Blue House.

In the late Joseon period, trade and commerce grew increasingly, markets were spotted everywhere and the ports of the Hangang River where overflowing with goods and merchants. In the late 1800s and early 1900s, new means of transportation such as cable cars and trains started appearing and homes began using electricity and communication devices such as telephones. However after the Japanese occupation of Korea in 1910, Seoul became a principal city that merely implemented Japan's colonial policies for 36 years.

After experiencing the Korean War(1950–1953), Seoul became a city of ruins. But after the 1960s, armed with the fast-developing Korean economy, Seoul also started to develop rapidly. Hosting the 1988 Summer Olympic Games and the 2002 FIFA World Cup events were great opportunities for Seoul to become a worldwide known city.

1. Doseongdo, a painting of Seoul during the Joseon Dynasty(1392-1910). As seen from this old picture, Seoul is surrounded by mountains and fortresses.
2. Namsan's beacon mound.
3. A general view of Seoul and Seoul Tower from Mt. Namsan.

ⓒ Choi Hang-young

ⓒ Yonhap News

Nature

Bukhansan National Park. Seoul is a special city thanks to this National Park and it is truly lucky to have Mt. Bukhansan (837m). There are very few cities in the world lucky enough to have a beautiful and magnificent mountain such as Bukhansan within their city. Mt. Bukhansan is located in the northern part of Seoul. Half of it is located in Seoul and the remaining half in the Gyeonggi-do Province. The area is 8,000 hectare. At the foot of the mountain lies a forest and the top of the mountain an enormous granite peak stands tall. Mt. Bukhansan is like a pair of lungs of Seoul. An average of 5 million people climb it annually. There are more people visiting this National Park per unit square meters than anywhere else in the world according to the Guinness Book of Records.

Mt. Bukhansan changes color according to the season. Until the Joseon period(1392–1910), people said that tigers lived in Mt. Bukhansan. But today only small animals such as deer, wild boars, badgers and lynxes live there. In this mountain, you can find a mountain fortress wall that is 9 kilometers long. Baekje was the first to build a fortress in this mountain. In 132 AD, Baekje built a mud fortress to protect its capital Seoul, from enemies. Joseon tore down this wall and built a stone fortress instead (1711). Most of this stone fortress remains today.

In Seoul, there are other mountains besides Mt. Bukhansan which embrace Seoul like a fortress. In short, Seoul is a city of mountains.

4. Mt. Bukhansan. These mountains are called "the lungs of Seoul".
5. Beautiful autumn leaves in Mt. Bukhansan.
6. Seoul residents climbing Mt. Bukhansan in the winter.

Hangang River. The Hangang River has always been Seoul's most important means of transportation. Here *Han* means "expanse and sacred water streams". The Hangang river originates from the mountainous mid-east section of the peninsula, passes through the Gangwon-do and Chungcheongbuk-do Provinces, crosses the middle of the Gyeonggi-do Province and Seoul and finally drains into the Yellow Sea. It is 514 kilometers long and the fourth longest river in the peninsula. The width of this river flowing through Seoul is around 1 kilometer wide and is larger beyond compare to London's Thames or Paris' Seine River.

The Hangang River divides Seoul into North and South. The northern part of the river is the "old city". *Cheong Wa Dae* (The Blue House), the official residence of the President, government buildings, embassies from around the world, palaces from the Joseon period, national museums and the Seoul City Hall are all found here. As a result, the southern part of the river is the "new city". Most of this region was developed after the 1970s. Large-scale apartment complexes, streets with fashionable clothing stores and commercial districts are the core of this section in Seoul.

Today's Hangang River possesses a greater meaning as a resting space for Seoul citizens than for its natural surroundings. On the shores of both sides of the river you can find grass turfs, swimming pools, parks equipped with gyms and soccer fields and also a jogging and bicycle course. A sightseeing ferry boat runs regularly on this river. At night, tourists and lovers ride the ferry boat to admire the night view of Seoul and the Hangang River.

7. Every October, a festival of fireworks is held on the Hangang River.
8. Seoul residents having a good time surfing on the Hangang River.
9. Night view of Seoul and Hangang River.

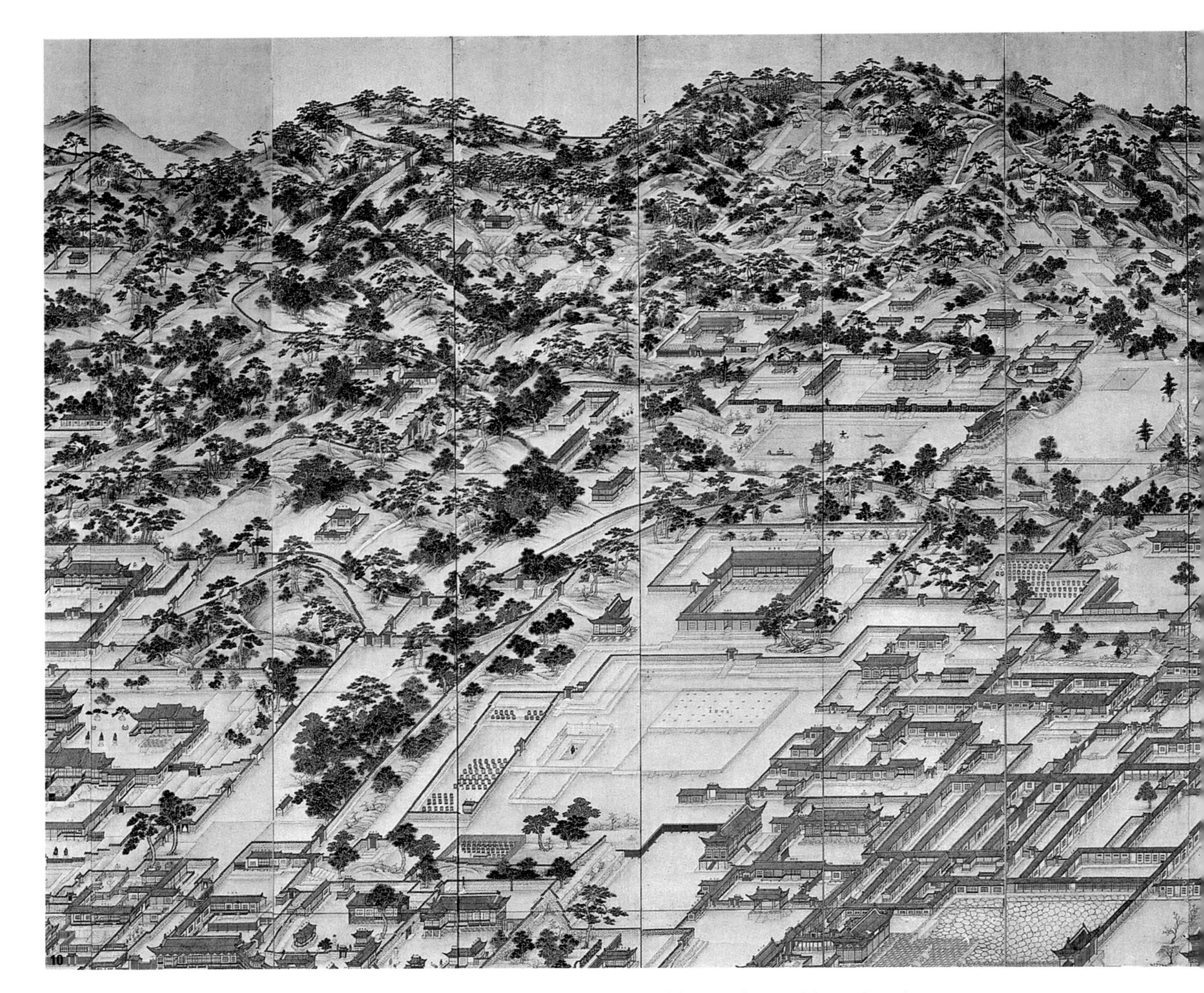

10. Donggwoldo (273cm × 576cm), a picture of Changdeokgung Palace and Huwon (The Rear Garden) from the Joseon Dynasty, National Treasure No. 249, Korea University Museum.

Royal Palaces
One of the characteristics of Seoul is that tradition and modern life are combined with harmony. The most traditional image of Seoul are the palaces of the Joseon Dynasty(1392–1910). There are five palaces in Seoul and these have become hot spots for foreign tourists who visit Seoul.

Gyeongbokgung Palace. This is the first palace to be built among the palaces in Seoul. General Yi Seonggye, founder of Joseon, built a palace at the foot of Mt. Bugaksan (now the mountain presently located behind Cheong Wa Dae, the Blue House) in 1395 and called it Gyeongbokgung Palace. However during the *Imjin Waeran* Wars in 1592, this palace was burnt to the ground. In 1868, after remaining neglected for 270 years, starting with Geunjeongjeon (National Treasure No. 223) or the throne Hall, all the buildings were rebuilt. Gyeongbokgung Palace was also greatly damaged during the Japanese colonial period(1910–1945). Japan partially tore down the palace and built its colonial governor's office inside. In order to restore the national morale, the governor's office buildings were entirely torn down in 1996.

Changdeokgung Palace. This was built as a secondary palace to Gyeongbokgung palace in 1405. Because it is located at the east of Gyeongbokgung Palace, it was also called the "East Palace". During the *Imjin Waeran* Wars, it

was almost burnt down to the ground along with Gyeongbokgung Palace, but was soon rebuilt. Until 1868, when Gyeongbokgung palace was rebuilt, Changdeokgung palace was used as the main palace of the Joseon Dynasty. Behind Changdeokgung palace there is a beautiful garden. Because this garden is hidden behind the palace, it was called "it *Huwon* or Rear garden". This is a typical garden that shows how restraint of artificial beauty was maximized in Joseon architecture. UNESCO acknowledged the architectural value and unique style of this palace and its garden and designated it a World Heritage. The painting that helped determine and decide Chandeokgung Palace and Huwon to be named World Heritage is *Donggwoldo*(literally East Palace drawing).

Deoksugung Palace. This palace is located next to the Seoul City Hall. It used to be much larger than it is today but after experiencing the Japanese occupation and the Korean War, many of its building disappeared. From the late 18th century to the early 19th century, there were many foreign embassies including The British, American, Russian and Belgian embassies clustered around Deoksugung Palace.

Apart from this, Changgyeonggung Palace was built in 1483 and it is located next to Changdeokgung Palace. Generally, the king's mother and grandmother resided here. And west of Gyeongbokgung Palace is Gyeonghuigung Palace which was built in 1617. Because it is located east of the Gyeongbokgung Palace, it is also called "West Palace."

11. Night view of Gwanghwamun. Front entrance of Gyeongbokgung Palace in Gwanghwamun.
12. Aerial view of a part of Gyeongbokgung Palace.
13. Reenactment of a traditional royal Korean wedding during the Joseon Dynasty.

14. Exterior of the War Memorial in Yongsan, a perfect place to learn about the history of Korea's wars including the Korean War(1950-1953) at a glance.

Museums

The National Museum of Korea. If you wish to know about the 5,000-year history and culture of Korea, you must visit the National Museum of Korea. The 140,000 cultural heritages show a detailed display of how Korea changed, from its past to the present today. A new modern building for this museum is currently being built inside the Yongsan Family Park. The size of the new museum building site is 30 hectare, and the building plot for the museum is 4.5 hectare. The galleries are divided into the Time Period Gallery, Theme Gallery and Outdoor Gallery. In the Time Period Gallery you can view the cultural heritages of every time period, from the prehistoric age to the modern age. This will greatly assist you in grasping an idea of each time period. In the Theme Gallery, Korean traditional art works are mainly displayed. The main galleries are the Buddhist Statues room, Metal Work room, Art room(calligraphy and drawings), Goryeo Celadon room and Joseon Celadon room. In the Outdoor Gallery you can see pagodas, Buddhist statues and stone cultural heritages of national treasure level.
The National Museum of Korea has divisions in 11 cities including Daegu, Gyeongju, Gongju, Buyeo, Gwangju, Jeju and Chuncheon.

The National Folk Museum of Korea. If you want to know about Korean folk culture and traditions you must visit the National Folk Museum of Korea found inside Gyeongbok-gung Palace. The National Folk Museum of Korea displays the Korean people's work and entertainment, clothes and

food, life and death in four different exhibition galleries. The "Hall of Korean Lifestyle" is a restored display of all the Korean traditional lifestyle, from prehistoric age to the Joseon Dynasty. By looking at the food, dwellings, dress, religion, architecture, language and scientific technology of the time, we can glance at how Koreans used to lived in the past. The "Hall of Koreans at Work" gives us a chance to see for ourselves what Koreans did to acquire materials that were needed for their lives. The "Hall of a Korean Life Cycle" is a showroom that displays all aspects of a Korean's typical life. You can get a glance at the rites and coming-of-age ceremonies a Korean typical person undergoes when he is born, studies, gets married and dies. The open-air exhibition of farming culture and old streets is also quite fascinating. Straw thatched-homes and mud houses, sheds, water mills, rice paddy fields and farming fields, late 18th century marketplaces and a typical 1960s Korean rural village have all been restored.

The Seoul Museum of History. The Seoul Museum of History is found next to Gyeonghuigung Palace. This museum arranged and displays all of Seoul's history and culture from prehistoric times to the modern day.
This museum will answer questions such as how Seoul has developed, how residents of Seoul live, what daily life inside a Joseon palace was like, what type of culture has flourished in Seoul, etc. You can also experience the "Touch Museum", a room that lures sightseers to make or touch products that old Seoul citizens used fishhand.

15. The National Folk Museum of Korea. This museum shows the lifestyle, tradition and folk culture of Koreans.
16. A Silla Kingdom golden crown, Treasure No. 338, The National Museum of Korea.
17. Geumdongbangasayusang, Gilt Bronze Sitting Meditating Buddha is kept in the National Museum of Korea. This Buddha figure symbolizes the artistic style of the Three Kingdoms Period (18 BC-660 AD). National Treasure No. 78.

18-19. Namdaemun Market and Namdaemun Gate. Namdaemun was formally called Sungnyemun. Sungnyemun means "Gate that values etiquette".
20. Dongdaemun Gate and Dongdaemun Market. Dongdaemun was formally called Heunginjimun. Heunginjimun means "Gate of uplifting mercy".

Shopping

Namdaemun Market. Namdaemun market is called this way because it is located next to Namdaemun(literally "Great South Gate"). In the year 1414, it opened its doors to the public offered by the government on a rent-basis, which means it has a 600-year history. It is the most representative traditional market of Korea when it comes to history, scale and functions. It has more than 10,000 stores and sells more than 1,700 types of items. Its main items are clothing and textile, kitchenware, ceramic pottery, local products, accessories and imported goods. Hence it has become a must-see travel destination for foreign tourists.

Dongdaemun Market. This market originated in the early 18th century. This market is called this way because it is located next to Dongdaemun(literally "Great East Gate"). After the mid 1990s, however, several big and modern shopping malls started setting foot in this area. Now the old traditional markets and the modern shopping malls can be seen side by side. Youngsters who are sensitive to fashion trends frequent Dongdaemun market. Because the modern shopping malls are quick to pick up on the customer's needs and put new items on the shelf. This is another travel destination where many foreign tourists drop by for a visit.

Myeong-dong. Myeong-dong, which means "bright village" is located very close to Namdaemun market. This is the most famous and popular fashion street in Seoul. The mobile population reaches 1 million people daily. Gathered in the streets, you can find department stores, clothing and shoe stores, restaurants, coffee shops and souvenir shops for tourists. This is another popular shopping destination for by foreign tourists in Korea. There are two fashion festivals held in the spring and fall in Myeong-dong.

Insa-dong. Insa-dong is a street of art and a traditional street that represents Korea. This street originated in the early Joseon Dynasty and mainly middle class residents dwelled here. Even then, it was already a center for artistic activities. Many *hanok* or Korean traditional houses, stores selling arts and crafts, antiques, traditional foods, tea and pottery, souvenirs for tourists and old books as well as several art galleries can be seen clustered in Insadong. There is no other place in Seoul where you can sense Korean tradition and culture as much as Insa-dong.

Itaewon. Itaewon is another shopping street that represents Seoul. Because several foreign embassies and a US Army Base are situated along this area, more foreigners live here than in any other place in Korea. You can see many billboards and signs in English. In Itaewon, you can enjoy shopping and entertainment at the same time. More than 1,000 various stores are gathered here. The majority of these stores sell clothes, leather goods, accessories and souvenirs. There are also diverse foreign restaurants, live music bars and coffee shops.

20

SEOUL
WELCOMES
THE WORLD

21

FIFA Confederations Cup Korea/Japan 2001
FIFA FAIR PLAY
HYUNDAI

22

21. Seoul Square filled with cheering fans during the 2002 FIFA World Cup. A view of Deoksugung Palace on the left.
22. Football game being played at the Seoul World Cup Stadium in 2002.
23. Fish sculpture displayed on the financial streets of Yeouido.
24. POSCO building in Teheran-ro, a prominent business street in Gangnam, Seoul.

Seoul Today

Sejongno Avenue. This is the broad street that starts from Seoul City Hall and leads up to Gyeongbokgung Palace. During the Joseon Dynasty, government offices were lined up on both sides of this wide street. Even now, the main government offices, ministries of foreign affairs, culture and information and technology are nestled here. Yesterday and today, Sejongno has been the heart of Seoul. This street received the world's attention due to the millions of cheering football fans gathered in the street during the 2002 FIFA World Cup event. In the summer of 2002, hundreds of thousands of people went out into the streets in red T-shirts to cheer for the Korean football team. Because of the World Cup, Sejongno has become the 21st century acropolis of Korea.

Yeouido. Previously, Yeouido used to be just a beautiful island in the Hangang River. Now it is the political and financial center representing Korea. Both the National Assembly and the Korean Stock Exchange are located here. Almost all the stock companies and bank head quarters are gathered here, making it "the Wall Street of Korea". In the middle of Yeouido lies a very big park. This park used to be an airfield until the 1950s when it was turned into a theme park. The park is divided into a Korean traditional forest, a grass lawn and an ecological forest. A pond and a traditional summerhouse are also found here.

Teheran-ro Avenue. Teheran-ro is the urban district's main street in the southern part of the Hangang River. It was named Teheran in the 1970s in an effort to develop friendly relationships with Iran. Here you can find a trade exhibition center, City Air Terminal, large conglomerate buildings, foreign corporations, hotels and department stores.
Under the Trade Exhibition Center and the City Air Terminal, lies COEX Mall, an underground city. Here you can find a cineplex, huge bookstores, a large aquarium, trendy and budget restaurants, fashion stores, coffee houses, and bars.

World Cup Park. This park was made for the 2002 FIFA World Cup event. Until the 1990s this place was a landfill where garbage and leftovers of the city where left discarded, a sign of over-consumption and abundance of city dwellers. Ten years since then, Seoul has made a beautiful park out of this landfill they had neglected and left in ruins for so long. Here you can find the World Cup Main Stadium where the opening ceremonies of the World Cup where held as well as a public golf course, a promenade (course), ponds, gardens, forests, an open air concert hall, ecological river, campsite, and an inline skating course.

KTX(Korea Train Express) and Seoul Station. The high speed train or KTX began construction in 1992 and was completed 12 years later in April 2004. It travels up to 350 km/hr and has 18,200 horsepower. There are two KTX routes, the Gyeongbuseon line connecting Seoul and Busan and the Honamseon line connecting Seoul and Mokpo.
The buildings of Seoul Railroad Station were rebuilt when KTX opened to the public. They were built in the shape of a bow. Next to the KTX Station is the old Seoul Railroad Station, a Renaissance-style building with a Byzantine dome built in 1925. This modern building sitting next to the old building is quite an eye-catching sight.

Busan

1

Area 762km2
Population 3,740,000
Location 445km southeast of Seoul
Temperature Average annual temperature is 14.4°C, January average temperature 3.0°C, August average temperature is 25.7°C

2

ⓒHyundai Heavy Industries

History

Busan is an international port city located at the southeastern tip of the Korean Peninsula. The first human presence in Busan goes back to the Neolithic Age. Ruins from the Bronze Age can be found in many places. Since 100 AD to 600 AD Busan belonged to the Gaya culture but later was incorporated in the Silla culture. The famous Haeundae and Dongnae natural spas can be found in this city. These spas have been famous since the 6th century. Kings, poets and nobles from Silla used to travel on holiday to Busan and visit these spas. These spas are regularly mentioned in the literary works of Goryo(918-1392) academic scholars.

Busan has been a port city since the 15th century. It did most of its trading with Japan. Commerce with Japan was so active then that Busanites prepared accomodation in a separate building for Japanese merchants. However Japanese people were limited from moving in and out of places other than the dwellings they were designated to stay at.

Busan emerged in the front pages of history and began shaping the foundation of the big city it is today 130 years ago. After it entirely opened its port in 1876 and signed a treaty with Japan, Busan became the most representative port city in Korea. During the Korean War in 1950, it became the provisional capital city, a period when Busan began to develop very quickly. In 1955, its population increased to over one million people and as the Korean economy started growing more and more rapidly, Busan became an increasingly international port city. During the 2002 FIFA World Cup and the 2002 Asian Games, Busan grew to become a world-class city.

Industry

Busan is Korea's most representative port as well as a city of logistics. Busan, which became Korea's first international port in 1876, is still a hub city of exportations and the center of the fishery industry. After preparing the basis for a good harbor in the 1940s, Busan started growing very quickly. It is now the 4th largest port city in the world. In 2001, Busan's port became the 13th port in the world to house a London Metal Exchange (LME). Also, part of this port city, measuring around 400,000 pyeong(approximately 1,322,320 square meters) was designated a duty free area since January 2002. The Busan port is continuing to grow even at this very moment. A complex logistic facilities, financial center, marine product processing area, international marine product exchange market and an international ocean center are under construction or expected to be built

1. Dongnaebu Sunjeoldo, a documentary painting depicting Joseon soldiers fighting against Japanese soldiers to protect Dongnaeseong Fortress during the Imjin Waeran Wars (1592-1598). Dongnae was Busan's former name.
2. A large ship sailing on Busan shores.

3

© Busan metropolitan city

4

5

6

© Yonhap News

© Busan metropolitan city

soon. When the Busan port expansion project is completed in 2011, Busan will grow to be the most modern port and logistics city in the world. Apart from this, shipbuilding, marine, tourism and car industries are core businesses for Busan.

Tourism

Haeundae Beach. Haeundae Beach is the most famous beach in Korea. The oval-shaped white sandy shores are very beautiful. It is perfectly equipped with hotels, spas, casinos and recreation facilities. Cultural events, sport competitions and festivals are held every season. On top of the 250-meter high Taejongdae you can see the beautiful view of the beach. Halfway up the mountain there is a 4.3km long roundabout. If you follow this road, you can see some steep cliffs and glance at the blue ocean. There is also a ferryboat pier near this area. The view from the ferryboat of Taejongdae cliffs and the pine forest is breathtaking.

Temples and Islands. Beomeosa, located in Mt. Geumjeongsan, is the most famous temple in Busan. Built in AD 678 it is one of the ten most famous temples of the Silla Kingdom. This temple's three-storied stone pagoda, sarira pagoda, Maitreya Buddha statues and bells have been named National Treasures. Geumjeongsanseong Fortress is a fortress that was built during the Three Kingdoms Period(18 BC–660 AD). It was originally 17 km long but only four kilometers of the original fortress remain today. Eulsukdo Island is at the mouth of the Nakdonggang River, a vital area for Busan. The river and the ocean meet here, an area filled with endless fields of reeds. These fields are the nesting ground for local birds. Every season, around 200,000 migrant birds and local birds visit this area because of its abundant foods, mainly ash trees, fish and sea food.

Jagalchi Fish Market. The Jagalchi Fish Market, with more than 480 stores, is one of Busan landmarks and the largest seafood market in East Asia. Every shop is filled with freshly caught fish and dry fish sea products. With countless street stalls, street vendors and raw fish restaurants the streets are always full of life. The Jagalchi Fish Market is a place where you can feel the special and unique charm of this beautiful port city.

Festivals & Events

The Pusan International Film Festival. Busan is a city of films that represent Asia. The Pusan International Film Festival has played a central role in publicizing Busan as a city of films. This film festival has been hosted every fall since 1996. The festival lasts for ten days, with participants from 60 countries around the world and plays 240 films. More than 5,000 people involved in the film industry are invited from Korea and all over the world. It is estimated at least 300,000 people visit this film festival annually. In addition, while this festival is hosted, Asia's biggest movie market opens its doors.

The Busan International Biennale. Busan is also a city of art. Since 1998, the Busan International Biennale has been held from May to October in every even-numbered year, an event that has made Busan a city of art. The Contemporary Art Exhibition is held in the Busan City Art Gallery while the Busan Sea Art exhibition, an installation art exhibition, and the Busan Sculpture Project, an exhibition that changes venues every year, are all held in Busan for around 150 days. Besides this, the Busan Sea Festival, the Busan International Rock Festival, the Sunrise Festival, the Busan International Motor Show and other variety of events, festivals and exhibitions are held all year round.

3. A scene of the Busan International Motor Show.
4. The official poster of the 2004 Pusan International Film Festival.
5. An installation work displayed during the 2004 Busan Biennale held in the fall of 2004 at Haeundae Beach.
6. The Busan International Trade Exhibition Center(BEXCO). Numerous banners inform of trade fairs and industrial exhibitions.
7. Jagalchi Fish Market, the largest fish market in East Asia.
8. Busan port at a distance.

1

Daegu

Area 885km²
Population 2,540,000
Location 302 km southeast of Seoul
Temperature Average annual temperature is 13.7°C, January average temperature 0.2°C, August average temperature is 26.1°C

History

Daegu is Korea's third largest city. People inhabited this area since the Neolithic Age. Dalgubeol, the first tribal nation of this region appeared during the first century. The present day Dalseong Park was the center town of Dalgubeol. Dalgubeol means "wide flatlands with great hills" and Daegu contains the same meaning. Daegu started developing rapidly after the governor's office of the Gyeongsang-do Province was moved to the city of Andong in 1601. The Governor's Office of Gyeongsang-do Province has controlled the administration, justice and military systems of the province for 300 years and have also prepared the basis for Daegu to grow as a major city in Korea. Daegu is an old city with a unique culture whose history goes a long way back. With the 2002 FIFA World Cup Korea/Japan and the 2003 Summer Universiade games, Daegu has also grown into a world-class city.

Industry

Daegu is the most famous city of textiles and fashion in Korea. The textile industry was the engine for the Korean economic growth during the 1960s and 1970s. In the 1980s the textile industry withered down due to the development of the machine, chemicals and electronic industries. However, starting in the late 1990s, Daegu began to grow once more as the textile center of Asia and with the implementation of the "Milan Project" it is gradually regaining its old period of prosperity. The "Milan Project" benchmarks Milan, a worldwide famous city of fashion and textiles and plans to transform Daegu's textile industry into a high value

2

© Daegu metropolitan city

added industry. Fashion shows and fashion seminars, exhibitions and fairs continue to be held all year round. Other than the textile industry, machine, metal, Oriental medicine and automobile industries are currently leading the economy of Daegu.

Tourism

City Tour Bus. The most effective way to sightsee Daegu is to ride the City Tour Bus. This way you get a chance to thoroughly see the main historical sites and museums, markets, temples and nearby tourist attractions. The most popular destinations in Daegu are Gyeongsang Gamyeong Park, a restoration of the old Provincial Government which existed 300 years ago, Dalseong Park, a park put in the central village of the tribal nation, Duryu Park with its diverse amusement facilities, Yakjoengolmok (Herb medicine market street), Daegu's largest market called Seomun Market, Donghwasa, a temple built 1500 years ago, Palgongsan, the highest and most beautiful mountain in Daegu, the Daegu National Museum where you can glance at Daegu's history and Daegu World Cup Stadium where a few soccer games were played during the 2002 FIFA World Cup.

Experience programs. Another attractive point about traveling to Daegu is that you can experience their Buddhist culture and have the chance to make kimchi by yourself. Through the Buddhist culture experience program, you can learn about the tea ceremony,Seon meditation and also taste temple food. If you choose the kimchi making experience program, you can learn how to make Korea's most prominent fermented food. You can also try bulgogi and kimchi.

1. Daegu World Cup Stadium.
2. Panorama of Daegu Tower and downtown Daegu.
3. Daegu's most prominent temple, Donghwasa Temple in Mt. Palgongsan, built in 832.
4. Fashion shows are held frequently in Daegu, which is dubbed the "city of fabrics".

Incheon

Area 954km²
Population 2,590,000
Location 30km Southeast of Seoul
Temperature Average annual temperature is 12.8˚C, January average temperature -2.4˚C, August average temperature is 24.9˚C

1. Exit platforms at Incheon International Airport. Incheon International Airport is the most prominent hub airport in East Asia.

History

Incheon is a large city located at the midwest section of the Korean Peninsula. Being adjacent to the Yellow Sea, Incheon is Korea's gateway to the world. In Incheon you can find the largest international airport in Korea and the second largest port. Incheon's former name was Michuhol. The ancient kingdom of Baekje(18 BC-660 AD) was actually formed in two countries. Onjo established a nation in present-day Seoul, while his older brother Biryu made a town(village) in Incheon and called it Michuhol. Soon Biryu's Baekje became annexed to Onjo's Baekje.

When Incheon port opened its doors to foreign nations in 1883 it became the gate for incoming western goods. From this moment on, Incheon begun developing rapidly as a port city. Incheon became known around the world because of the Allies' Incheon Landing Strategy during the Korean War in the 1950s. It also became a world city when the Incheon International Airport opened its doors in 2001 and during the 2002 FIFA World Cup Korea/Japan celebrations.

Industry

Because Incheon is an excellent port, several industries have developed balancedly including, refined oil, steel, automobiles, electric, machine and furniture industries. After the Incheon International Airport opened its doors in 2001. Incheon has been pushing its way to become the hub city of Northeast Asia. Incheon has all the means and elements to become a "penta-port" with air, sea, telecommunication means, business, leisure resorts, etc.

Songdo is a new informatization city with teleport functions and is under construction at this very moment. Yongyudo and Muuido are two beautiful islands close to the Incheon

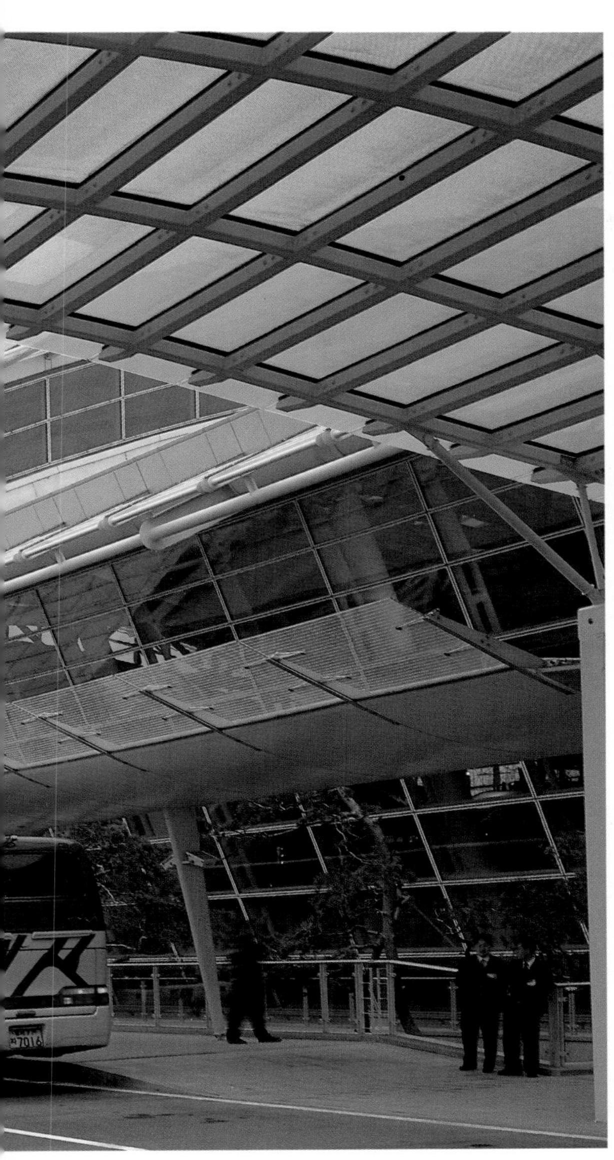

shores that are being developed as tourism, culture and leisure spots. In addition, a Business Port is set to be open on an economic free zone centered on Incheon International Airport.

Tourism

Wolmido. Wolmido used to be an island but later its shores became landfills connected to the mainland, it became land. From 1920~30s it was one of the most beautiful recreational parks in Korea. Now it is a place of romance and culture visited by many young people. On side is the sea while the other side is lined with cafes and seafood restaurants. The sunset is the most charming present Wolmido gives its visitors. The red sun that goes down in the sea is a magnificent sight to see.

The Incheon Grand Park also greets its visitors with a different color and smell at every change of seasons.

Ganghwado Island. This island is like a historical documentary film. Relics and cultural artifacts from the Prehistoric Age to the modern age can be found here. For example, dolmens, mountain fortresses, temples that have been built more than 1,000 years ago, Goryeo Dynasty(917 – 1392) temporary palaces, Anglican churches built as *hanok* (Korean traditional house), and 19th century's remains of national defense facilities. When looking at Ganghwado Island, it feels like watching a scene from a documentary film. Ganghwado is famous for producing large quanitities of Insam. Everywhere you go you can see Insam fields and at the central village of the island you can see very big shopping malls that specialize in selling Insam.

2. A sculpture of General Douglas MacArthur's displayed in Incheon Freedom Park. General MacArthur made a successful Incheon landing operation during the Korean War.
3. Chinatown, Incheon.
4. Night view of Incheon International Commercial Port.

Gwangju

Area 501km^2
Population 1,400,000
Location 300 km Southeast of Seoul
Temperature Average annual temperature is 13.8°C, January average temperature -0.1°C, August average temperature is 26.3°C

1. Ipseokdae Rock in Mt. Mudeungsan symbolizes the city of Gwangju. Climbing this mountain guarantees a fantastic view of Gwangju.

History

Gwangju is the most principal city of the southwestern region. Gwangju means "city of light" in Korean. It functioned as the main city of the southwestern region since the Christian era. During the Baekje period, it was called "Mujinju", but during the Goryeo Dynasty(918-1392) its name was changed to Gwangju. Gwangju is a sacred ground for Korea's democratization. During the Japanese Colonization Period, this region had the most active independence movements and was also the leader of the Korean democratization after 1970. Particularly in May 1980, this became the shrine for democracy after the Gwangju popular movement. Gwangju citizens rebelled against the military government to fight for democracy, justice and defend their freedom and human rights.

Since long ago, Gwangju has been the home of culture and art. Highly learned seonbi(Confucian scholars or masters), poets and painters were born in this city. Gwangju is the hometown of Korea's traditional paintings. Every other year since 1996, the city has been hosting the International Biennale.

Industry

Gwangju has developed focusing on administration, education and culture. However, since the 1980s, the second generation industries have greatly developed. Befitting to its name, which means "the city of lights", Gwangju has intensively nurtured the light industry. Design and cultural contents industries are all receiving attention. This is because the central and local governments are

© Gwanju Biennale Foundation

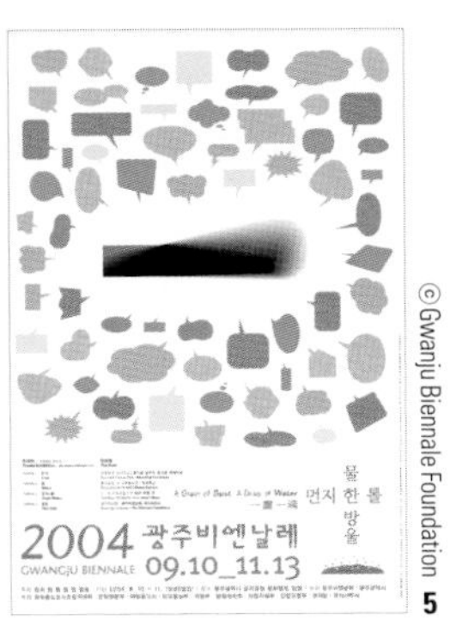

© Gwanju Biennale Foundation

2. An ancient tomb found in Bannam-myeon, near Gwangju.
3. View of a tea farm in Boseong, near Gwangju.
4. Art works displayed during the 2004 Gwangju Biennale in subways.
5. The official 2004 Gwangju Biennale poster.

joining forces and carrying out projects to make Gwangju a cultural city that well represents Asia. Starting with construction of culture complex centers such as the Paris' Pompideu Center, Culture and Arts, Specialized Graduate schools, design centers, culture industry specialized complexes are expected to be built soon. A few years from now this city will have culture and art festivals all year round along with the Gwangju International Biennale and the Design Biennale.

Tourism

Mt. Mudeungsan. Mudeungsan is the most famous mountain in Gwangju. It is located at the far east section of Gwangju. It stands 1,187 meters above sea level. In the spring, rhododendrons and azaleas, in the autumn fallen leaves and purple eulalias and in the winter snow covered trees landscapes are beautiful sights to see Ipseokdae, Seoseokdae, and Gyubong summit are three of Mudeungsan's most picturesque views. Square, hexagonal and cylindrical shaped 20-30 meter high stone pillars stand tall like shrines.

Gwangju National Museum. At the Gwangju National Museum you can glance at all the traces of Gwangju cultural heritage from the remote prehistoric age to the present day. This museum was built with a Korean traditional architectural roof tiles. You can also look at not only this reqion's relics but also famous ceramics of the Joseon and Goryeo Dynasties and ceramics brought across the Yellow Sea from the Song and Yuan Dynasties of China.

Daejeon

Area 539km²
Population 1,440,000
Location 160km Southeast of Seoul
Temperature Average annual temperature is 13.28°C, January average temperature -1.7°C, August average temperature is 24.4°C

1. Daejeon, Korea's seventh largest city, as seen from a mountaintop.

History

Daejeon means "large field" in Korean. It is Korea's seventh largest city. Humans started living in Daejeon since the Paleolithic Age. However, the one moment in history this large field became the center of Korean history was back in the early 20th century. Daejeon was just a quiet rural area back then. But in June of 1904 a railroad connecting Busan and Sinuiju in North Korea started construction and this is when Daejeon started growing as the most prominent city of the central region of Korea. This is because this railroad's most important train station was built in Daejeon. Daejeon started growing rapidly in 1932, after the administrative offices of Chungcheongnam-do Province were moved from Gongju, Baekje's ancient city to Daejon. Daejeon is also the administrative city that has the 3rd Government Buildings Complex in Korea. It is also famous for its hot springs. At the same time it is a city of science that has led Korean science research since the mid 1970s. In short, Daejeon is the most rapidly growing city in Korea.

Industry

Daejeon is the science and technology city of Korea. Daedeok Science Town in the outskirts of Daejeon has approximately 230 universities, government and private companies' research centers including the Korean Advanced Institutes of Science and Technology(KAIST), the Korea Atomic Energy Research Institute(KAERI), the Korean Bioscience and Biotechnology Research Institute(KBBRI) and the National Science Museum. These research centers and universities are the strong pillars supporting the advancement of Korean science and technology.

Daejeon is a dynamic city that is second only to Seoul for having the most venture companies. More than 800 venture companies are found here and they are gathered mostly in the Daedeok Science Town. Not far from now, these venture companies will become the leaders of Daejeon and Korea's future economy. Already many venture companies are cooperating with universities, research centers in developing new products and commercializing them. The Daedeok Science Town is the most exemplary science and technology cluster in Korea.

Tourism

Daejeon's most famous tourist sites are Mt. Gyeryongsan and Yuseong Hot Springs. Mt. Gyeryongsan is the most famous national park in the central region of Korea. "Gyeryong" means "chicken and dragon" and this mountain was given this name because the top of the mountain resemble the chin of a rooster and the slopes of the mountain resemble the body and tail of a dragon. This mountain is famous for its many temples including a temple that is 1,600 years old called Gapsa Temple.

People started visiting Yuseong Hot Springs 600 years ago. The founder of Joseon dynasty(1392–1910), General Yi Seonggye, stayed to relax in the Yuseong Hot Springs when he came to inspect Daejeon more closely. Back then Daejeon was one of the strong candidates for the country's capital city. Other notable destinations are the Daejeon Zoo, Expo Park, Daejeon World Cup Stadium. The City Tour Bus is a convenient way to sightsee Daejeon's tourist sites. The City Tour Bus has one daily tour taking you to see all the sites mentioned here including Gongju, Baekje's old capital city.

2. The EXPO Park. The tower seen in the back is Hanbit (Great Light) Tower, a symbol of Daejeon.
3. A dome-shaped star-gazing chamber inside the Daejeon Observatory.
4. Research scientists of the Daedeok Science Town absorbed in an experiment. The Daedeok Science Town is a prominent scientific city in Korea.

Gyeongju

Area 1,323km²
Population 290,000
Location 372 km Southeast of Seoul
Temperature Average annual temperature is 12.4°C, January average temperature -1.5°C, August average temperature is 25°C

1. Chilburam Maebul, Seven Buddhas Hermitage, Mt. Namsan, Gyeongju. (8th century). Treasure No. 200.

History

Gyeongju is the most prominent city of Korean cultural heritage much like Athens is for Greece and Rome is for Italy. Before the Three Kingdoms Period (18 BC–660 AD), there was a tribal nation named Saroguk inside Gyeongju. Later Saroguk became Silla (57 BC–935 AD). Gyeongju was the capital of Silla for almost 1,000 years. Gyeongju is almost a time capsule of history in that it is filled with Silla's cultural heritages, ruins and artifacts.

Walking down the streets of this city, you can often meet up with hill-like royal tombs and also find pagodas and temples everywhere. Gyeongju developed even more rapidly after Silla conquered Baekje and Goguryeo and succeeded in unifying all Three Kingdoms (676). This is because Silla accepted the more advanced Baekje and Goguryeo's culture, technology and political system. Most of Gyeongju's representative cultural heritage were produced at this time in history. In 935, Silla surrendered to Goryeo(918–1392) and gave its place as capital city of this 1,000 year-long kingdom to Gaeseong. During the Goryeo Dynasty, many people from Gyeongju worked in politics so the city enjoyed a great deal of benefits as the third largest city after Gaeseong and Pyongyang. However it did not get much attention during the Joseon Dynasty(1392–1910). In the recent years, Gyeongju has become the city of history in Korea again and furthermore gained attention as a city of

history all over the world. All of the central district of Gyeongju is a national park. More than 7 million people visit this city to see Silla's cultural heritage each year. More than 100 relics have been designated National Treasures or Treasures.

World Heritage

Bulkguksa Temple and Seokguram Grotto. Befitting a worldwide known city of history, Gyeongju has two UNESCO cultural heritages. First is Bulkguksa and Seokguram, considered to be the essence of Buddhist culture and second is the Gyeongju Historic Areas. Compleleted to build in 774, Bulguksa is located halfway down Mt. Tohamsan, southeast of Gyeongju. It is a very unique temple that embodies the profound Buddhist ideal or the paradise and ideal world described in the Buddhist scriptures in its architectural structure. This type of temple is hard to find in Asia, an area where Buddhism has flourished extensively. There is artistic beauty in the shapes of each and every one of the pagodas of these temples, reinforced stone walls, bridges, and inner temples. Along with Bulguksa, Seokguram is the best Buddhist work of art made during Silla Kingdom's height of prosperity. Seokguram is a natural stone that was trimmed into a dome-shaped cave where a statue of Buddha was placed inside of it. It is a monumental Buddhist sculpture that achieved success in the aspects of architecture, mathematics, geometry, religious passion and artistic spirit altogether.

Gyeongju Historic Areas. Gyeongju Historic Areas contains the history and culture of Silla Kingdom's 1,000 year reign(57 BC – 935 AD). The historic areas can be divided into five sections according to their characteristics-specifically, the Namsan area which gathered pagodas and Buddhist figures in an open air museum, the Wolseong area or the location of the palaces of this millennium lasting royal dynasty, the Daereungwon area which contains royal tombs and stone mounds gathered, Hwangnyongsa area which shows the characteristics of national Buddhism and the Mountain Fortress area which has the defense facilities for the capital city. Historic areas of Gyeongju are considered to have excellent and diverse historic sites higher in density than the ones in Kyoto or Nara in Japan.

2. Areal view of Daereungwon Tomb Park and Gyeongju. An impressive view of numerous hill-like tomb mounds in the middle of the city.
3. A Silla Kingdom tile with patterns of smiling faces.
4. A stone figure of an Arab warrior guarding a Silla Kingdom King's tomb. This proves that Silla was a nation active in international trade.
5. Cheomseongdae, the oldest oriental astronomical observatory, was built during the early 7th century. National Treasure No. 31.

3

4

5

Gongju

Area 940km^2
Population 132,000
Location 143km South of Seoul
Temperature Average annual temperature is 11.8˚C, January average temperature -0˚C, August average temperature is 24.1˚C

1. Donghaksa Temple in Mt. Gyeryongsan, Gongju.

History

Gongju was Baekje (18 BC–660 AD)'s second capital city. After Goguryeo (37 BC–668 AD) invaded and conquered Seoul, it moved its capital city to Gongju in 475. The name of Gongju was Ungjin back then. Gongju was very suitable for a capital city because it was surrounded by mountains and also because Korea's fifth longest river, Geumgang fended off enemies. Baekje moved its capital city to Buyeo 63 years later.

Many Paleolithic Age artifacts have been found in Gongju and it is belived that this is because many people relied on the river for survival. Gongju was a very important city during the Goryeo and Joseon Dynasties. During the late 19th and early 20th century, it served as the provincial government of the Chungcheongnam-do Province. In 1932 the provincial government moved to Daejeon and hence passed on its function as the central city in the middle region of the peninsula to Daejeon. However, in 2005, Gongju was named one of the candidates to be Korea's administrative city and is expected to have a splendid and magnificent comeback.

Tourism

Royal Tombs. In Songsan-ri, the vicinity of Gongju, lies Baekje's royal family's tombs. Among these, the tomb of Baekje's 25th king, Muryeong (r.501–523) has very high historical value. It was discovered in July 5, 1971 as an intact stone mound. The stone epitaph said the people buried inside the tomb were King Muryeong and his Queen, which was exciting news for everyone. In this tomb, archeologists found more than 2,906 relics of 108 types including the royal

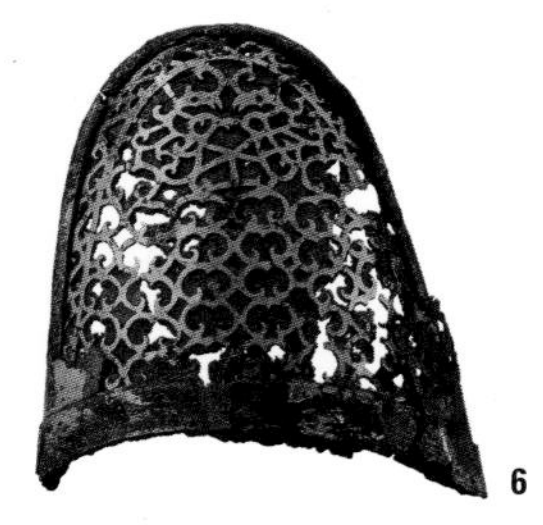

crown. Of these, 17 relics were appointed national treasures. King Muryeong's tomb is registered in the potential list of World Heritages.

King Muryeong bestowed a bronze mirror to the 26th king of Japan Geitawa and one of King Muryeong's direct descendant became the 50th king of Japan, King Ganmu. King Akihito acknowledged this fact a few years ago. Because of this history, on August 3, 2004, one of the uncles of the king visited the royal tomb of King Muryeong to pay him respect.

Gongsanseong Fortress. There is a very large fortress in a small mountain at the shores of the Geumgang River in Gongju. This is where the Gongsanseong Fortress of the Baekje Royal Palace. Gongsanseong Fortress was its name during the Joseon Dynasty but was called Ungjin Fortress during the Baekje Period. Unfortunately, only some traces of a pond and the location of Baekje's royal palace can be found. The structures and fortresses we see today are those that have been restored according to historical records. The fortress is around 2.2 kilometers long.

Museum. The most famous relics are the ones excavated from King Muryeong's tomb. The relics shows who is buried in the tomb with memorial stones, coins, bronze mirror, gold- plated shoes, golden crown, large sword with a dragon and phoenix carved on it signifying the king's authority and power and numerous accessories such as earrings demonstrating the high quality of arts and craft works of the Baekje Period, some 1,400 years ago.

2. Aerial view of Gongju.
3. Gongsanseong Fortress. of the Baekje Royal Palace.
4. Gapsa Temple in Gongju, built 1,500 years ago.
5. Gold crown ornaments found in King Muryeong's royal tomb.
6. Gilt bronze hat excavated from King Muryeong's royal tomb.

Buyeo

Area 624km^2
Population 87,000
Location 155km South of Seoul
Temperature Average annual temperature is 11.8˚C, January average temperature -0˚C, August average temperature is 24.1˚C

1\. Gungnamji Pond in Buyeo was built during the Baekje Kingdom(BC18-AD660).

History

Buyeo is a small and quiet city located just fifteen minutes by car from Gongju. Buyeo became Baekje's third capital city in 538 after Gongju. After Baekje established its capital city of Buyeo, it founded a cultural nation that achieved a balanced development in the political, religion and artistic realms. In addition, Buyeo also passed on many of its advanced culture and civilization to Japan and played a crucial role in contributing to the shaping of ancient nations in Japan.

However, Buyeo also is a sad city that contains all the pain of Baekje Kingdom's downfall. Choi Namseon, a famous writer from the early 1900s wrote, "Solitary and blue, in and out, all solitary and blue is Buyeo". In AD 660, Buyeo surrendered its royal palaces to the allied forces of the Silla and China's Tang Dynasty and sadly faded from history.

Tourism

Royal Tombs. At Neungsan-ri in Buyeo there is an ancient tomb park where kings and royal tombs are found together. There's a total of 7 tombs and they all face south with mountains situated at their backs. The tombs are crescent-shaped. It looks as if a green colored moon is half sticking out of the ground. The tombs are not overpowering or authoritative. However grave robbers stole from these tombs and therefore the identity of the people lying there is still unknown. In 1993, the Bronze-gilt Incense Burner, one of the masterpieces of Baekje's metal crafts was dug out of this temple nearby this ancient tomb park.

Pagoda. There is a 1,400-year old pagoda standing in an

empty temple in the center of Buyeo. This is National Treasure No. 9, the Jeongnimsa site 5-storied Stone Pagoda. This is a stone pagoda in the form of a wooden pagoda that shows the process of the wooden pagodas changing into stone pagodas. This is the second oldest stone pagoda of the 1,000 stone pagodas in Korea. It is 8.8 meters tall. The pagoda seems soft but firm, strong but elegant. Its imposing height, decent and upright look and intellectual appearance are like emotions felt when looking at a beautiful woman. When seemingly useless stones meet a person's wisdom and craftsmanship, a beautiful work of art is born.

Museum. In the Buyeo National Museum you can see the relics of the Baekje culture at its height of prosperity. The most beautiful relic of these is Bronze-gilt Incense Burner. It is 62.5 centimeters high and is composed of three parts: base, body and a lid. At the top of the lid is a phoenix spreading its wings as wide as possible and flying away with a magic stone, the dragon ball under its mandible. In the middle of the lid are carved 74 mountain peaks, 39 animals, and musicians playing instruments. This incense burner expressed the union of Taoism and Buddhism into formative plastic art. It is a superb work of art that shows excellent creativity and dynamic energy. The minting and plating technology are impressively accurate and meticulous. This is considered to be a masterpiece and the most beautiful incense burner discovered in East Asia. In addition, other aspects of Baekje can be appreciated through such excavated items as potteries, Buddha's figures, metal crafts and stone sculptures.

2. Baekje's royal family tombs in Neungsan-ri, Buyeo-eup.
3. Jeongrimsa site 5-storied Stone Pagoda was designed like a wooden pagoda. National Treasure No. 9.
4. Bronze-gilt Incense Burner. National Treasure No. 287.

DMZ and JSA

Area 1,517km²
Location Longitude E 38

DMZ
Korea's Demilitarized Zone (DMZ) is located at the center of the peninsula at the E 38°··· parallel. It is 250km long, east to west and 4km wide, north to south. It is around 1,571 square kilometers in width. The DMZ is a land of sadness for the Korean people. It was delimited after the truce of the Korean War in July 1953, that has separated Korea into South and North.
After 2000, a great change occurred in the DMZ. In June 15, 2000, the first South-North Summit Meeting was held after the division of the nation. Because of this, the doors of the DMZ that had been shut close for 50 years were slightly open for limited areas. Now on the east and west end of the DMZ, a railroad and highway are busy under construction. Temporary roads have already opened. Through this temporary road the south and north carry goods. Also, people from the South can visit Mt. Geumgangsan through the temporary east end road. The DMZ which had been a symbol of division has now transformed into a crossroad of exchange, reconciliation and unification.
For more than 50 years, almost no human had set foot on the DMZ. Thanks to this, the Korean people received an unexpected asset. The DMZ had become a land of rare life forms. Various types of plants, animals, birds, insects and fish are found living here. This was a playground and refuge for internationally protected animals, endangered animals and countless natural treasures. Today, the DMZ is an ecological treasure and a paradise for wild animals and plants.

Panmunjeom
This is the Korean name for the Joint Security Area(JSA) inside the DMZ military demarcation line. It is located 48 kilometers northwest of Seoul and 10 kilometers southwest of Gaeseong. Panmunjeom is the window that notifies the world of the situation in the Korean Peninsula. The year after the Korean War began, UN and North Korean military forces built a few straw thatched-houses and started negotiating an armistice. After agreeing on a truce, the UN and North Korean forces appointed this place a joint security area and each side put several guarding soldiers. Panmunjeom is a narrow space having a radius of only 400 meters from the demarcation line.
After the armistice was agreed upon there was an exchange of POWs. After the Armistice, Panmunjeom was used mainly as the truce management location but after the Red Cross Preliminary Talks were held in September 20, 1971 it became not only a place for the Military Armistice Committee meetings but for contact and talks between the South and the North. It has also been used as a transit point when passing from and to the South and North. Before 1976, the South and North could freely go to and from the South and North side of the demarcation line inside Panmunjeom. Strong tension and a mood of silence always flowed in Panmunjeom. However after 2000, an ambience of reconciliation has spread throughout this area and the expressions of the JSA soldiers and the faces of the guarding North Korean soldiers looking to the South have softened. Along with the DMZ, the JSA is a symbol of the divided Korean Peninsula. Today it is not filled with guards but has become a crowded place with curious tourists sightseeing the South's side of the JSA.

1. South Korean soldiers checking the barbed wire in the DMZ.
2. Panmunjeom seen from the South Korean side. North Korea supervises the gray building seen at the top of the picture.
3. Barbed wire fence installed along the mountain ridges of the DMZ. The left side of the barbed wire fence is North Korean territory.
4. Rusted helmets and boots used in the DMZ.

Index

The Discovery of Korea

First Edition **2005. 1. 30**
Second Edition **2005. 10. 15**
Third Edition **2007. 3. 15**

Text by **Yoo Myeong-jong**
Photo by **Kwon Tae-kyun**

Translation **Paik Un-he, Debora Paik**
Design **Park Young-mee**
Publisher **Yoo Myeong-jong**
Published by **Discovery Media**

Registration Number **22-2486**
Registration Date **February 11, 2004**
807, Daewoo Officetel, 1328-75, Seocho 2-dong, Seocho-gu,
Seoul, 137-858, Korea
Tel **82-2-587-5558**
Fax **82-2-588-5558**

Printed in Korea

ISBN 978-89-956091-0-1 03980

About the Authors

Yoo Myeong-jong is a poet and a critic of culture. He majored in Korean Literature at Korea University and held the post of senior reporter at the monthly "Literature and Thought", the monthly "Roots and Wings", and editor-in-chief of the prestigious "Morning Calm" magazine. With much interest on the history of cultural exchanges he frequently contributes articles on Korean cultural heritage to several magazines along with photography and painting masterpieces. He has also published "My heart rests when I hear your voice", a poetry book.

Kwon Tae-kyun is currently in charge of the Photography Team at the Current Affairs Media Department of Joongang Ilbo, one of the major daily newspapers in Korea. He majored in Photography at Joongang University and worked as a photojournalist at the monthly "Saemmi keepun mool" (Water of a deep well). Since 1982 his works have been centered on Korean history, culture, and the daily lives of Koreans. He lectured in History of Photography and courses of documentary photography at Joongang University and Sangmyeong University, and has participated in five major exhibitions.